LOOK BOTH WAYS BEFORE
BREAKING THE LAW

Sophia Echeverria

Cover design and book layout by Rebecca Woods

Address correspondence to:
Sophie Echeverria
P.O. Box 546
Moulton Loop
Jackson, Wyoming 83001

LOOK BOTH WAYS
BEFORE BREAKING
THE LAW

A ROWDY MEMOIR

by

SOPHIE ECHEVERRIA

Wickenburg, Arizona and
Jackson Hole, Wyoming

Dom Echeverria, Navy Air Corp

DEDICATION

Look Both Ways Before Breaking the Law is dedicated to Dom Echeverria, who provided our family with The Worst and The Best of Times.

The Worst were precipitated by Dom's penchant for keeping us perched on the precipice of peril, as he did indeed break laws, not always looking both ways first. His fiery Basque temper too often nearly knocked us over the edge, and his unpredictable behaviors kept us in chaos.

The Best of times were that we learned how to survive disasters and to be joyful despite whatever befell us. Mostly. Dom gave us wonderful, wild adventures and he surrounded us with the beauty of our ranches and of the lands he acquired for our sheep, cattle, horses, dogs, cats—you name it, we probably had it. We are grateful for what he achieved as one of the ten largest sheep operations, and the largest producer of fine wool, in all the USA. His success provided homes we loved, excellent schools, and much that was truly good. Celebrate gratefully we must.

So here's to you, old Dom! I dedicate to you what follows *When in Doubt, Step on the Gas*. Good Heavens, you are probably flipping in your grave....

ACKNOWLEDGEMENTS

Susanne Walsh, with her brilliant insights, memory, and ability to make my computer behave is really my co-author. For several months she was absorbed in opening her new shop and could not help me. Serendipitously, Nate Cook, a professional editor, arrived on my doorstep with my grandson, Otto Hanson. They were to visit for five days, but they became so involved in helping me with the book they stayed for five glorious weeks. Together we managed to finish this book, or we almost finished it. My sons and daughters, who asked to remain unmentioned (cowards), then added new insights and tales which add greatly. Thanks, family.

Our Wyoming Writers' group and our Annual Jackson Hole Writers' Conference has been wonderfully helpful, especially Tim Sandlin, Linda Hazen, Larry Reiser, Lyn Dalebout, Lori Gunst, Katie Ives, Mike Bressler, and indeed, our entire group. My gratitude is profound. All of you have been better than a PhD college course in writing. You have taught me so much, and your encouragement has kept me going. Thanks.

Gratitude for my family, friends, and Dom Echeverria himself, overflows, as you are the ones the "shaggy saga" is about. Without you, my life would have been horrendously boring. Thanks, dears!

TABLE OF CONTENTS

PROLOGUE:

ICE CREAM IN JULY

Good heavens! As I write the rowdy saga of the Echeverrias, I wonder, did all that really happen? Clearly memories of times long past are so unreliable that I may be venturing into hot water. It seems we all believe what we believe subjectively, and our recall is colored by our own unique circumstances, personalities, and needs. Then we cheerfully see those whose memories contradict ours as deluded, or even nuts. Memories are like ice cream at a July picnic. They kind of ooze into a mess. Yes, I may be in hot water.

Take my youngest brother Dana for instance. From the time he could talk until his teens, he believed he had been on a vacation to Maine with our parents, my baby brother John and three-year-old me. "Don't tell me I just imagined that lake, and our log cabin! I can still see the daddy long-leg spiders that crawled up the walls!" he would say. Then we would put a dent in his little soul by telling him, "Dana, you were not even there!" He was born five years after John and was not yet even a lusty gleam in our dad's eyes when we made that trip. He had heard enough, and he had seen so many pictures of North Pond and the log cabin, rustic and full of daddy long-leg spiders, that it became quite real to him, confounding us all.

I remember that trip too. Dad took me canoeing and I longed to go again. One afternoon I escaped and made it to the canoe all by myself. Joyfully I cast off and floated out among tall reeds and into the vast and shining lake. Dad spotted me and ruined my adventure. Darn! Like Dana, had I just imagined it? Later I came across a picture of me out there on North Pond, so I did not imagine it. Why had Dana? Our minds are a mystery.

Accepting that mysterious minds produce memory that is slippery sets me free to write whatever seems best to preserve our history. As there can be no light unless there is dark, bravely I have included some of our considerable difficulties, but the ultimate aim is to give you, dear reader, a good time. Of course, I responsibly search for the truth, though I will not fall off my stool in astonishment if anyone disagrees with my version of events and characters.

My husband Dom's first five years of college were financed by the GI Bill, earned through his time in the Navy Air Corps. It took him through two years each at the University of Arizona, the University of Colorado, and Colorado A&M, but still he had three more years to go to earn his degree as a Doctor of Veterinary Medicine.

It was when Dom and I were students at the University of Arizona that we met. He was so darkly good-looking and intelligent I was swept away. My Kappa Alpha Theta sorority sisters asked, "Where did you find such a gorgeous man?" He apparently was swept away by me, too, to my amazement. We were married in 1948, and moved to Boulder, Colorado, where he continued his studies.

I worked, but my earnings barely kept us going. We finally managed those last years by pooling our meager resources to buy 246 old ewes. Both from ranching backgrounds, we knew how to make our "woolies" turn enough profit to sustain us. We had no land of our own, so we moved our sheep from rented farm to leased ranch, wherever Dom could find pasture. Constantly on the move, our lives, though exciting, became chaotic.

Good Catholics that we were, we had eight children in twelve years. (Catholic birth control did not work, thank God. Not one would I "return to sender.") First, Elaine, then Jack, who died when he was only fifteen months old of Cystic Fibrosis, next came Peter, Paul, Anne, David, Sophie, and finally Joseph. Both Peter and Joseph, like Jack, inherited Cystic Fibrosis.

Our tribe of children and I lived a gypsy life as we followed Dom, tending our livestock over far-flung ranges. Adventure and excitement lit up our lives and more than made up for some horrendous difficulties. Cystic Fibrosis is a terrible, always fatal disease. We struggled to live fully in spite of it, providing our seven children with all the fun and wild adventures we could possibly create.

During the school year we couldn't follow Dom as he traveled with the livestock, so I was too often a single mother. As Dom's partner in both his practice of veterinary medicine and the sheep and cattle enterprises, I was so busy I could not achieve the order and attention to parenting that was needed. Control? Out of! We often seemed about to crash into something ominous, and to sink, gurgling, to some dark bottom. A little snort, a glass of Port, and we lurched forward, by golly, and survived. Great love, and our gift of laughter, often outrageous, carried us through. Sometimes it almost did not.

Here is more of the story.

THE BASQUES: PROUD REBELS

Dom Echeverria was born in Northern Spain, in the Pyrenees Mountains. Basque, he inherited who he was, and who he was, was something else. That something else sometimes overwhelmed us. Dom found a ranch to lease in southwestern Wyoming near the Flaming Gorge that promised a summer of good grazing. Grass, green and lush, waved in the Wyoming wind that swept in from the Uinta Mountains towering in the West. Red rock ridges rose to embrace the meadows. Stands of aspen and pine clustered in little forests provided shade and shelter. We parked a Wyoming sheep wagon at the edge of an aspen grove for Marcello, the Basque herder who was to be in charge of the two thousand sheep soon to arrive on big semi-trucks.

All was ready, the sheep were unloaded, and Marcello followed them, his Border collie, Chowdie, at his side, prancing happily, and ready to keep the band in order. They streamed through sage sprinkled meadows, making sheep music as ewes and lambs called to each other. Their backs undulated in a kind of river as they trailed up into the shade of the aspen and pine groves, munching sweet grass and wild flowers along the way. Birds sang announcements that their territory was being visited, and a group of elk bounded off in alarm. We felt no guilt about encroaching on their territory, as the land we had leased was but a Band-aid sized patch on the vast wilderness. Dom had followed the truck loads of sheep and taken two of our sons, Pete, eleven years old, and Paul, eight, with him. When they returned home, Pete, with trembling voice, told me what had happened.

He said that his Dad was hell bent on poaching an elk. That is not a way of cooking, it is the act of shooting game out of season, a punishable felony, but Dom did not bother with little formalities like laws. He needed meat for our thirty-four sheepherders and our large family. He grabbed his guns, jumped in his Ford pickup truck and yelled, "Get in the back boys, and climb up on the racks so you can help me spot game!"

Pete, small and thin, with cystic fibrosis, described how he and little Paul hung on for dear life as his Dad hit sixty miles an hour, across open land, bouncing over sagebrush and gullies. Pete choked out what happened next. "Dad spotted some elk and swerved the truck real fast to get a shot at them. Paul was thrown down into the bed of the truck and hit his head on the metal rod of a tire jack. I jumped down off the rack and had to pull hard to get his head unstuck and off that jack. Blood began to spurt out of the hole, and I thought for sure he would die!" By the grace of God, really a miracle, it had not penetrated his brain. Pete said he pounded on the truck cab yelling, "Dad! Stop! Help!

Paul is unconscious and bleeding to death!" I could picture Dom as I had seen him often, his eyes glittery and glued on those elk, so intent he would not even think of slowing down. Pete said he just threw a box of Kleenex into the back of the truck and yelled, "Stuff it with this!" so he began frantically packing tissues in the hole.

My heart broke, as I listened to Pete, so frail, so sad and so scared, but heroic in the way he had "hung tough" and saved Paul's life. Then I imagined Paul unconscious and bleeding. He was a beautiful little boy, with black hair, dark eyes, and a sparkling personality. Both he and Pete were "creatively daring," and added much to the tumult of our lives, but mostly they brought joy. Paul was nicknamed "The Terrible Tempered Mr. Bang" but he called himself, when he was little, "Boy Nice," as that was what he wanted to be. It fit, as his charm and his inherent good heart won him friends and compensated for the temper that caused the "bangs."

Guardian angels surely with them, Pete managed to stanch the flow. Finally, Dom drove up to Marcello's sheep wagon and put Paul, unconscious, on some wool sacks stacked nearby. "I don't want blood all over the camp, so keep him out here," he told Pete, as he jumped in the truck and sped away, leaving the boys alone. Dom, with his degree in veterinary medicine, and his years of experience with ranch accidents, had to have known the injury would not be life threatening. Even so, such behavior left scars on my psyche, and most likely on Paul's and Pete's.

Pete said he could hear the sheep nearby and ran to get

Marcello. He took one look at limp, bloody, little Paul and lifted him into his sheep wagon. He washed off the blood, patched the wound as best he could with his first aid kit, and eventually Paul came to. Marcello made chicken soup and fed them sheepherder bread. Pete remembered it gratefully for the rest of his short life, and Paul says he remembers that wonderful soup and bread to this day.

It was many hours and pitch-black dark when Dom finally picked them up and made the long drive home. I took Paul to our friend, Dr. Haley, at the crack of dawn. He admired how Marcello had patched the wound up and asked who he was. I told him, "He is Basque, a friend, almost part of our family. He lost an arm in a sawmill accident and lacking access to medical help, he had to take care of himself. He learned from wise old Basque women how to treat injuries. He's our hero. He saved Paul."

Paul said, regarding the hole in his head, which as it healed grew a bright patch of white hair amidst his black, "I haven't been the same since." He has "never been the same since" with shocking frequency, his whole life one disaster after another.

The same thing happened again on another ranch, near Wheatland in eastern Wyoming. At that time, no one had crew cabs; the kind of pickups with small back seats and it was the usual thing for kids to ride in back, hanging on to stock racks. Another sharp turn, and again it was Paul who was smashed into the bed of the truck, another piece of equipment jabbing a hole in his young head.

Paul's head must have been a prime target for Dark Forces or was he just accident prone? The kids were playing on a haystack and he fell off, landing on a pitchfork. Dave yanked it out, and the kids all stared in astonishment and horror as four spurts of blood shot out of four holes. Guardian angels rescued him yet again.

A Cultural Legacy

The Basque way of handling things often threw "normal" folks into tizzies of disbelief and shock. I was shocked numb; stunned into silence by how Dom dumped Paul and Pete out by a pile of wool sacks with Paul's head gushing blood. Silently I agonized over his behavior, wondering how in the world he could have done that. Then I recalled things he had told me about his culture and childhood that gave me a somewhat ameliorating perspective.

The Basques were the first people indigenous to the Iberian Peninsula, thought to have originated with the Neanderthals, as there are similarities in their skull structures. It is thought Cro Magnon man may have eliminated the Neanderthals. New theories emerge adding to the mystery that surrounds their disappearance, but whatever happened, whether they preceded the Basques or not, the Basques lived on. Tough and inventive, they overcame the Cro Magnons, survived everyone else, and are the only race to inhabit what is now Spain continuously. They stubbornly resisted occupation by wave after wave of invaders, including centuries of Moorish occupation. Meld with the Moors? What a horrible prospect! Bow to the Romans? Absolutely not! However, they were crafty enough to lure the invaders into business arrangements that enabled them to glean from the occupiers a lot more than they wanted gleaned. The Romans gave up and left.

The pride for which the Basques are famous served them well in that it kept them racially pure, "unsullied" (as they would see it) by mixing with anyone not Basque. They have also maintained their culture, largely unsullied, by rigorously obeying their fueros, laws carved in granite for millennia.

The result of their rigidity was inbreeding that produced a 60% incidence of RH-negative blood and a high infant mortality rate. Despite that, the pride that forbade marrying out of their race perhaps could be seen as similar to the selective breeding that is done to produce superior livestock. Basques, as a race, are generally strong, athletic and intelligent. Their pride in who they are and their accomplishments is unshakable, and it is well earned. It also protects them from having to admit to a "few little shortcomings." They tend to violence, they can be cruel, and they kill with impunity.

There is firm evidence that they were the first Caucasians on the American Continent. Their "Lauburu," the iconic Basque symbol, has been found carved in stones in the northern parts of the United States. The four arms curve gracefully in a swastika-like pattern, each symbolizing their four Earth elements: wind, sun, water and fire. It is believed their skill and daring in fishing and whaling brought them here.

Basque bankers, miners, fishermen, and industrialists are so aggressive and bright that, with the Catalonians, it is said they control two-thirds of the Spanish economy. Their culture has produced composers, musicians, dancers and artists, and of course some of the best sheep men in the world. Out of that culture came Dom Echeverria, with innovations all his own. Dom inspired me to learn everything I could about his race. Kind reader, if you are interested, I refer you to *A Basque History of The World* and The University of Nevada, at Reno, has a fascinating Basque studies program.

Who was Dom Anyway?

Dom wrote his own rules with no regard for the government and he had no intention of bowing to social customs he thought lacked practical value. Yet in his business dealings he was honest and likable. Ranchers, farmers and all with whom he dealt, trusted and admired him.

He raised our children to follow suit, which they did with alarming enthusiasm. In Dom's opinion, the advice he gave them was completely sensible. "Look both ways when you are going to break the law," he would say as he zoomed through stoplights, exceeded speed limits and hunted out of season. By the grace of God and faithful guardian angels, the children stayed alive and out of jail (mostly) as they followed their dad's example. Dom was even more independent than most Basques, and for him, fueros were for those folks in Spain.

His character was molded by his childhood experiences. Dom was thirteen when his father, old Miguel, sent him with a herder, some dogs, burros and about two thousand sheep up the dry Hassayampa River bed, past Remuda Ranch, and on to Burro Creek. They trailed the sheep for two weeks to the summer ranches forty miles west of Seligman in northern Arizona. Mountain lions threatened, and were shot, followed by coyotes, all hungry for sheep. Dom described the trips as harrowing and hard, but wonderful.

When he was just a little guy his dad had been to Seligman, in northern Arizona, for supplies and was headed back to their Cross Mountain Ranch. It was forty miles over a rough two-track dirt road and Mikel, twelve, the oldest son, was bounced out of the back of the truck where the numerous children were riding. Pounding on the cab roof and shouting did nothing. Miguel, rugged to the bone, thought they were just having fun and on he drove. When they arrived at the ranch house, the kids pointed out to him that Mikel was missing and had fallen out some ten miles back. He said, "Ten miles? He can walk home easy." Thank God nothing was broken and Mikel did indeed walk the ten miles, in the dark, bruised and sore, but he and everyone else seemed to regard the whole thing as pretty routine. Just don't fall out of the truck.

Affection was strangely lacking, despite warm and noisy good humor. Dom said he could not recall a single time his father or mother touched him with affection or expressed love. Indeed, his mother said she hated him and she abused him so badly, (she beat him with kindling wood) that he carried scars all his life and said the best day of his childhood was when he grew big enough to outrun her. He had justified anger buried in his soul, and there is no doubt

23

some of his cruel behavior came from that. His family didn't seem to think a thing about it.

One summer, Dom took Elaine, baby Jack and me to the Cross Mountain Ranch for a family gathering. As we headed out over the long, rough road an Arizona "frog strangler" came up, a major thunderstorm that dumped a ton of water in no time at all. A muddy flood swooshed down a big flat and over the road. Dom cheerfully said, "When in doubt, step on the gas," and off we went straight into the flood. The truck stuck fast, water swirling half way up the doors. "Well, darn, guess we will have to hike in. We're half way there, shouldn't be too hard," he sighed, not concerned at all about whether I could make it carrying little ten-month-old Jack. I chose to think that he so admired me that he had no doubt I could cope just fine. It was sort of a comfort to believe that. Halfway there? That would make it twenty miles to the ranch! He put his beloved little Elaine, two years old, on his shoulders and waded in. I picked Jack up, grabbed my little cocker spaniel Linda, and did my best to follow. Dom shouted over his shoulder, "If you get tired, just wait in the road. Someone will come and get you." And off they went.

Linda, brave little dog, swam frantically beside me as I plowed through waist high, muddy, swirling flood water, struggling not to let it knock me down with Jack in my arms. "Hey, Guardian Angels, COME!" I pleaded, and suddenly I felt miraculously strong, supported by something powerful, as I plowed on through. We staggered up the bank onto the road and began to hike. It was long after

24

dark when I finally gave out. I sat on the edge of the road, hugging both Jack and my little dog tightly for warmth. There was no danger that I would sleep and anyone who came for us would miss us, as Jack, frail and small was hungry, wet and cried pitifully. It seemed like a year before one of Dom's brothers turned up in a truck and took us to the ranch house.

Dom's fierce mother, Vicencia, greeted me with something like disgust, saying," You look awful," but then she gave me hot chocolate and some milk to fill Jack's little bottle and we headed for bed. No one thought the events of that day were at all unusual. The rain was wonderful and would bring great pasture for the sheep and cattle.

The Echeverrias just breezed through difficulties in their unique way. Everyone faces difficulties in an individual way, and I remembered how we did it. When the wimpy city children, guests on my family's Remuda Ranch where I grew up, whined over any little thing, like horse manure on their new boots, my brothers and I, tough little ranch kids that we were, looked on in astonishment. "What was the problem?" We had manure on our boots and Levis, too, and it seemed nothing to be bothered about. It is all relative, is it not? So I managed to become as high-dee-ho, yo-ho-ho as my Basque family and I was actually pretty darned proud to have made it through that storm without moaning even a little bit.

The "difficulty" of our trip through the flood and into the Cross Mountain Ranch was never to be forgotten, but how could I not rise above it when the rest of our time there was wonderful? Cross Mountain Ranch was beautiful, ruggedly spectacular, embraced on the south by the mountain for which it was named. Cross Mountain was a complex of granite mixed with volcanic extrusions that rose steeply into ridges that formed a huge cross. Airline pilots used it as a landmark. When we were in college and courting, Dom and I had ridden up it as far as our horses could go, and then hiked to the top. Some astonishing love- making had taken place up there. Oh my God, what a man! What a day! So there we were again, with wonderful memories.

And Who Are Those Kids?

The differences in Dom and me, cultural and temperamental, produced offspring who embodied a volatile mix of our juxtapositions. We could not provide a solid, united front as parents, and the kids had to emerge very much their own creative selves. Fireworks were inevitable. Here they are, briefly.

Elaine came first, born in Fort Collins when Dom was studying for his degree in veterinary medicine. Dark and beautiful, she was adored from the day of her birth, Dom's most Basque, most beloved daughter. Her great uncle, Pete Fletcher, said she looked like a rare flower and he named her The Peony Bush in the Garden after a hilarious song sung by comedian Danny Kay. Meanwhile, her great grandfather, Dr. Fletcher, said her eyes were so big and black she looked like a bug, and instead of The Peony Bush, her nickname was Bugsy Pal, hardly fitting for a child so beautiful, but it stuck for years.

Jack arrived thirteen months after Elaine, her little brother whom she adored. He was born with cystic fibrosis and was tragically ill from the day of his birth until his death when he was just fifteen months old. I carried him most of the time to try to ease his distress, little Elaine following, trying to be helpful. Between bouts of misery, the little fellow was a delight, with a merry smile and warm affection, happy to play with his sister. When he died, both Elaine and I were devastated. We had tried so hard to make his life bearable, and to save him.

Jack's life and death imprinted Elaine with a gift for caretaking. She nurtured her pets, she fussed over her friends when they were in trouble, and this lovely characteristic has remained with her. As a nurse, she was especially good with dying people and even nursed family members in her home, easing their ways to their deaths. She met the challenge with wonderful grace and skill.

As a very little girl, she learned to work hard at her father's side, both with the livestock, with our horses, and at home. We sent her to private school, Lincoln, in Providence, Rhode Island, where she somehow became awfully proper. I, her very own mother, have shocked her! As have her siblings, but she has a great heart and she loves us despite our lack of propriety. In fact, I think she loves it and slyly joins us in mischief. After all, she is an Echeverria.

The bond between Elaine and her father was so tight that she escaped the brunt of his destructive behaviors. She finds puzzling the pain and anger the rest of us feel about him, and our negative attitudes she sees as unfair. Considering who he was, and the harm he did, it is good. He has a champion and a defender, even if it confuses me.

Pete was born six months after Jack's death, also with cystic fibrosis. Early on he learned during hospitalizations and contact with other cystics that his life was tenuous, and that death was imminent. With passion he embraced all the life he could. Hypocrisy and waste of time infuriated him, and he blasted away at anyone or anything that didn't meet his standards. We had dinner at an elegant restaurant in Boulder when Pete was about ten and when his meal failed to please him, he loudly announced, "Take this crap back! It tastes like cat shit in a boot!" We wanted to escape, to pretend we didn't know him, but escape is hard if you can't stop laughing.

His attitude toward our Catholic church was pure Pete. During a stay in the Longmont Hospital, our old, staid parish priest paid his obligatory visit to the sick. He said, unctuously, to Pete, "You know that being a patient means being patient." Pete replied, "F-k off, Father!" Then the priest tried to give Pete Holy communion, possibly thinking it was almost time for Last Rites. Pete said, "Communion is holy only when bread is broken and wine shared among people who love each other." The priest slunk away.

The Longmont Hospital soon moved Pete from the usual double room to one of his own so we could set up his stereo equipment to provide him with his beloved music. Before the move, I came in one day to see Pete's bed closed off with curtains. Our family plumber was in the next bed, and said," Sophie, just leave! Don't open the curtains!" "Oh my God," I thought, "he's dead!" I opened the curtain, and there

Pete was, joyously having sex with one of his lovely girlfriends. The plumber was relieved when I closed the curtain and left.

Pete loved his siblings, but he hated his father, who scorned him as a weakling. His relationship with me was positively volcanic. Since it was I who was supposed to keep him alive, he was angry that I couldn't save him. Several times he threatened to murder me, furious at what he saw as my stupidity. Because Dom often yelled at me, "How could you be so stupid?" he was set up to think of me that way, as were his siblings, and blame stuck to me like tar and feathers. But there was another side to me, not at all stupid, and in fact, bright and funny, and when that side of me was allowed to come through, it and our shared love of books and good music would return us to each other.

That love of books and fine music brought Pete friendships with people who were definitely not the usual, more like fascinatingly weird. Their noses in deep tomes, classical music booming, they were definitely different. The usual kids caused great pain, and more than once Pete came home from St. John's School in tears because they called him pretzel legs, he was so small and thin. With fire and fury he reacted. Before being passionate was trendy, Peter was the embodiment of pure blazing passion. He hated and loved with all of his fierce and doomed heart.

Paul burst on our scene a beautiful little fellow, so full of curiosity and mischief he left me, his "old Ma", in clouds of dust. "Where's Paul?" On the roof, or up a mountain, or in a tunnel he dug under our house, or lighting a campfire with Peter under the bed? Attempts to control him were met with his explosive temper, and he deserved his title, "The Terrible Tempered Mr. Bang."

We lived on a remote ranch in the Peruvian Andes for almost a year when Paul was just under two. He proudly sat in the saddle in front of his dad on Dom's big, grey horse as they rode the mountains supervising thousands of sheep and cattle. The Indians who lived on the ranch thought little Paul was the greatest, and his life was loaded with fun and adventure. Then his big brother Pete became so ill I had to take the children and return to the United States.

Paul's "Boy Nice" blossomed in Arizona, and he beguiled everyone, but his Terrible Tempered Mr. Bang title stayed with him. The loss of his Dad, and our life in Peru, was devastating to him, and he dealt with his pain by becoming defiant. He fought for himself and his siblings. My family, intimidated by such a wild child, fervently wished we would leave Remuda. My grandmother, Clem Fletcher, said frequently, "I hate that child!" We had no place to go until Dom joined us fourteen months later when his contract was completed, so we were trapped, doing the best we could. Somehow that experience produced a kind of heroism in Paul. He battled for what he saw as right, determined to be a warrior, to defend us in any way he could. He has remained a warrior.

Like Don Quixote (my role model), Paul did noble battle for good. Thrice he saved kids from drowning, and on one terrifying day he managed to rescue his little brother Joe when he was trapped

31

under tangled wire in a rushing river. He saved deer and other wild-life hit by cars from agonizing deaths by euthanizing them by the side of the road. He carried a gun mostly for that purpose. He also put out numbers of fires started by careless tosses of cigarettes on roadsides. He has always been quietly amazing in the good he does. As with practically everyone in the world, he has a shadow side, and it has amazed us as dreadful events came to light, but he transcended them all and they contributed understanding and wisdom to the man he has become.

Anne, next to pop on the scene, was almost born on some wool bags out near our sheep as her dad had to check on a shearing crew on our way to the hospital. We just made it to a gurney, where Anne emerged as the first baby of the New Year. She has been first in just about everything ever since. A beautiful little person, we called her our precious Petunia, shortened to Tuny.

She was bright and mischievous from the beginning, with a wonderful curiosity. We had a wall-to-wall library full of the classics, the Great Books Collection, and an eclectic assortment that she began reading almost before she started school. She read her first Pulitzer Prize winner, Laughing Boy, in fourth grade. It was difficult to get her little snoot out of her books to help with all the work we shared around the house and ranch. The stories of the Saints, especially Saint Theresa, were favorites, so I stooped to Machiavellian tactics, and told her, "You know, Anne, St. Theresa loved to read too, but when her mother told her to do chores, she just put her book down and did what her mother asked." It worked, and from then on she was my dream minion. Oh goodness gracious me, sometimes the super-smart are so up in their heads they can be really gullible, and can be the last to see what devilish doings are going on. Anne (like her mother, I have to admit) often sailed along obliviously missing the gist of things.

There was a reason Anne was reluctant to help. She was terrified of Dom's dictatorial demands and the cruel way he treated her, so she created a hiding place in the back of her closet. Equipped with a lamp, blankets and pillows, it was a comfortable hide-away, completely undetectable from the outside. She could hear Dom's boots coming down the hall, as he snarled, "Where is Anne?" She barely breathed as he searched for her, never discovering her hideout. This went on for years. Meanwhile, I prayed he would not find her.

Funny, warm and charming, everyone but Dom loved her. With a mind and a curiosity as lively as hers, of course there was plenty of mischief. She tortured the nuns at St. John's with great heresies, and she and her friends rolled their uniform skirts up to daring heights, flirting outrageously with any boys who came their way. Early on, she had boyfriends. I was horrified, and I never gave up my motherly efforts to steer her in good directions. How did that work? Guess. Boredom? Not a minute. For all that, Anne negotiated the wild river of life, rapids and all, rather splendidly. What a trip!

Dave inherited a few characteristics from my family, thank heavens. After all the trouble I went through to have him, it would be sad if I didn't get at least some credit for how he turned out. He was born in the Wickenburg Jail, a distinction for sure. The new hos-

33

pital had been completed, everything but the delivery table had been moved and the old hospital had been converted into the town hoosegow. So there I was, giving birth to Dave in the Wickenburg Jail. It was a very difficult delivery, and had we remained in Peru as Dom had planned, to be delivered on the ranch like the Indian women were, we both would have died. How odd—we owe our lives to Pete's illness that sent us home.

While definitely Echeverria, Dave looked a little like my Dad with hazel eyes and brown hair, much lighter than Dom. Inheritance is amazing. Dave never knew my father who died long before he was born, but he had mannerisms like his; the way he moved his hands, and his wit and charm. Jack Burden (my father) exactly. He also inherited some of the brilliance his great grandfather, Dr. Fletcher was famous for, as well as Dom's extraordinary intelligence and facility with numbers. An adventurer and expert camper from the time he was six years old, he earned the nickname Davey Crockett that was later changed to Davey Cricket, more in tune with his whimsical side.

He had much to contend with, as Dom had a weird resentment toward him, much like the animosity he harbored towards Anne. Dave, even when he was quite young, scorned his father for that, and with vehemence and cleverness made his own way. I admired and supported him as much as I was able. Of course Dave was angry, and like Paul, he channeled it into his role as a heroic warrior for justice.

Over the years he became an expert on war, guns, and battle. I hated all that interest in violence, and consulted a counselor. He told me it was Dave's creative way of dealing with mountains of buried anger. He became such an authority that when he was in college, a professor in World War II studies gave up after a number of Dave's corrections, and actually asked him to conduct the class which he did with distinction. His degree, however, was in business agriculture with a minor in business law, and thanks to that education, he has been a tremendous help to the family over the years as we worked managing our Wyoming ranches.

Both Dave and Paul had a recklessness about them that resulted in many accidents and injuries. "Oh my God, what next" was a constant with me. Dave's wit was wry and sharp, and with it he developed a wonderful storytelling ability, fueled by plots that evolved out of his and Paul's wild adventures. There are wild books in both of them waiting to be written.

Sophie Dominik was born during cocktail hour exactly nine months after Dom's return from Peru. A bright little star, Dom named her Twinkle-twinkle soon shortened to Twinkie. Beautiful from birth, she beguiled us all. Except Paul and Dave, who, when they were about three and four, became so jealous of the love Dom showered on her that they conspired to do her in. "Let's push her down the stairs," they whispered, and then they did. Those stairs were made of flagstone, and due to the fact that Sophie was so tiny and so light and bounced, and that she had a guardian angel, she survived. She was bruised and in pain, but uninjured. What happened to Paul and Dave? I don't want to think about it.

Soph's mind developed a Quixotic originality from the beginning, and she loved drama. One day, when she was in second grade, she and her friend Dawn Peterson were playing happily in the room the girls shared. Anne burst in, demanding privacy, and a big fight developed. Unable to achieve civilized reason, I finally asked Dawn to go home, just a block away, for an hour to let the dust settle, and then come back. She didn't come back, and that night when I went to bed, pinned to my pillow was the following note:

A Sad Story

It was a cold day. I had just got home from school. I felt lonesum, so I invited my friend Dawn over. We were having a good time when allavasun my sister Anne came in. She made everything so sad! So I told my Mom. She didnte do a thing about it, eksept she told me to send my friend home. So I did. It felt like a prsen getting reddy to go on a trec across the desert, crunching in the ice and snow. Simed like going over the crunchy big rocks. It was so sad, IEL never frget it.

Her second grade writing and spelling were a little shaggy, but her passion, her drama, more than made up for it.

The nuns in St. Johns School called from time to time saying, "Mrs. Echeverria, you must DO something! Sophie is a HERETIC!" In the class on Catholic religion, each student was instructed to tell what he or she thought of God. "God is good," "God is kind," and so forth, until Sophie, frustrated beyond endurance, exploded. "What's wrong with you? You are talking about GOD! He is magnificent, all-powerful, beyond our understanding and you guys are sounding like Pablum!" She apparently peppered it with some expletives and was sent to Father Ron. I said something like, "Oh my goodness, I'll talk to her," but I had no intention of discouraging her.

I was proud of her and relished our shared rebellion against the things in our religion that just did not work for us, so our talks were hardly what the good Sisters had hoped for. Sophie was so adorable, and I guess I was enough of a holy challenge that they never gave up trying to save our untamed souls. Bless their hearts for such friendship and caring, but we remained untamed.

Joseph was our youngest, and as such was called Baby Joe. His brothers would not stand for such a demeaning title and declared, "He's not the family baby. As last in line, let's call him Joe Caboose." Like Jack and Pete, he was born with cystic fibrosis and his life was a struggle. Very early he realized that he was not long for this world and his feisty wisdom about it was an inspiration. "I have no time to waste on bull shit," he said, and woe to anyone who came across as fake or silly. He acquired fine books to add to our splendid library, reading as extensively, even the great Russians, and as deeply as Anne and David.

Joseph escaped the anger that Pete had and for all his intensity and insistence on maintaining the best and most beautiful in life, he was loving and good-natured. He said regarding his lack of anger, "Thank God dad died before he had a chance to ruin me!" What staggering insight in a little fellow! But as his disease impacted him more and more over time, he became sometimes desperate, and in that desperation, he could be very sharp. His siblings changed his nickname from Caboose to "Little Hitler" as he demanded what he needed, no matter what anyone else thought. There was resentment that I spoiled him, which I did indeed. I would not let cystic fibrosis ruin his life as it had Jack's and Pete's, if I could help it, which of course I could not. But I tried, and so with me he was wonderful. We shared a love of good music, good books, ballet, the symphony, and we were great friends.

Dom and Pete

From early childhood Pete had a sense of his destiny. He summed it up with a little poem:

Shoot for the moon
Shot from the Earth
Rocket Man
From the day of birth!

"Rocket Man" he was! Even with cystic fibrosis, Pete was a tough little guy, and perhaps a little mean. He beat up his siblings at any provocation. He also could keep up with all the work that had to be done despite his illness. His small being filled our lives with an intense energy.

Sadly, as Pete's illness took him farther and farther down, Dom began to turn away from him. Dom had a phobia about hospitals, never visiting if he could help it, and he could not deal with Pete's frequent hospitalizations. Also, sadly, he could not accept that he, Dom Echeverria, could have such a sickly offspring. Indeed, any weakness any of us revealed was intolerable. (Elaine was an exception. She did not experience this.) Fear was the result for most of us, and we conspired to hide problems from him, but for Pete, the result was fury. A Rocket Man who was to shoot to the moon, he was not about to sit still for the nastiness his father dumped on him.

His fury erupted terrifyingly; he swore as colorfully as the Spaniards, he drove hell bent for leather, shot his gun, and was prone to whacking his victim du jour with whatever weapon he could find while he heaped on verbal abuse. There were times his behavior so infuriated Paul that he considered murder. Always, thank God, Paul was able to pull back and see it for the tragedy it was.

Paradoxically, Pete could bounce from fury to wonderful joyousness, his humor and mischief lighting up our lives. He was a talented artist and expressed his life in his paintings. In one he stands holding a wine glass high, a bottle in his other hand, on the slope of a volcano that flowed red-hot lava and shot fire to the sky. Another shows a Pete-like person jumping over the moon, rabbits and birds as his companions. Then there are his ships, sailing toward his rising moon. He also wrote, but much of what he produced was so laced with swears and heartbreaking stuff that it is hard to read and not to be published.

Drumming was a release for much that went on in his tormented soul, and he was good. He also played the banjo, the piano by ear, and the harmonica, his musical talent a delight, but I thought, "Good grief, I'm going to lose my hearing!" Not only drums, all kinds of music rocked our home on its foundation. No way would I deny Pete or any of us the music we loved. Earplugs were out because mayhem and murder (really!) were always threatening, and I couldn't miss that. No wonder I'm "deef as a post" as they say, and have to crank up my hearing aids.

.

RANCH LIFE

⸻

Dom's family had acquired their four large ranches, two west of Wickenburg for winter pasture, and two in northern Arizona for summer grazing in the 1920's. I relished our visits to the summer place. The home was old and rustic, but it served well. The land was beautiful, with mountains, green pastures, pinion pines, groves of deciduous trees by a stream, well-tended gardens and an orchard of delectably laden fruit trees. Their livestock; cattle, sheep, goats, chickens and horses kept everyone busy. Milk was squeezed out of contented cows morning and night and left to sit until rich cream rose to the top and was skimmed off to make great desserts. The goats' milk was put in bottles with nipples so that the adorable orphan lambs who followed us around hoping we were their mothers could be bottle fed. The darned goats got into everything; they even climbed up on top of vehicles, leaving "calling cards." Some of our cars looked like Appaloosas, they were so polka dotted. Chickens cackled around the yard, helping with bug control and supplying eggs. The horses were beautiful and essential to managing the cattle but they had to be fed twice a day and left prodigious piles of manure.

This was a life I wanted for our children. Hard work that would build strength and competence coupled with a wild kind of freedom and a lot of laughter. The close bond with animals and the open land touched souls. It had made the Echeverrias strong and capable, they lived life fully, and how good that was. So what if there were aspects that were a little "difficult"! We were on a journey; a really different one from anything I could have imagined and I loved it.

Dom found a ranch near Parshall, Colorado, in 1964, and leased it. Lush stretches of grass spread over rolling hills with aspen and spruce groves here and there, dense, dark and alluring. As well as a livestock ranch, it was a famous guest ranch, The Buckhorn.

We had to be there to take care of the sheep for the summer, and happily we rented one of the little cabins that lined the creek. How delicious it was to sleep there, the river making river song, air fragrant and fresh. The guests were the same sort of nice people we had back on Remuda and we felt at home. (Among them were the Neusteters who owned a splendid store in Denver, where my mother bought her wedding wardrobe years before, and was now our favorite place to shop.) The dining room, with tablecloths and flowers, welcomed us. We loved being in a beautiful place with lively, bright people but we had little time for socializing. Several bands of sheep roamed the ranch and we needed to ride the range, herding them to water in the creek and keeping them under control to prevent over grazing.

Water for the sheep camps was hauled in big steel milk cans. One day Dom filled a number of them in the creek and loaded them into the back of his pickup. Paul, Anne, Pete and Dave were in the back, Elaine was in front with her Dad, Sophie and little Joseph were with me, ready to follow in the station wagon. Dom took off like a bullet just as a fisherman sped onto the bridge. "Stupid idiot!" Dom yelled, as he swerved to miss him and careened into the creek. The cans crashed violently, knocking the kids around the truck bed. One slammed into Dave, the sharp rim slicing across his little face. He gave a frantic yell as blood streamed down his shirt. Anne remembers feeling a sickening panic. I remember that feeling all too well also. Dom jumped out, picked Dave up and handed him to me, bloody and traumatized. "Take him to Parshall. There must be a doctor there somewhere," he ordered. With one hand I tried to stop Dave's alarming blood loss as I drove as fast as I dared to the little town. There was a doctor available, by the grace of God, and he closed the gaping wound with fourteen stitches from the bridge of Dave's nose almost to his chin. His eye barely escaped injury but then it swelled shut and turned black. It took a while but he healed well and has grown up to be handsome, scar and all. In fact, it lends mystery to him, hinting at his life of adventure.

Southern Colorado

Next season, we moved on to La Garita, a ranch in the San Luis Valley in southwestern Colorado with the Sangre de Cristo Mountains to the east, the famous Colorado sand dunes, where the children played, and the San Juan Mountains to the west. On our way to the ranch we picked up a hitchhiker, something we rarely did, as in the

Wild West, it was dangerous. (A rancher kindly rescued one in a blizzard and the hitchhiker killed and ate him.) This fellow looked like a professor with his grey beard and glasses and the boys had their pistols so we felt safe. We listened, eyes wide, as he told us about a peak that towered to the sky nearby. Pointing to it, he said, "Spaceships have a port there! I can hear their hum as they come in to land and as they take off! I am going to be ready for them next time they come." He was headed into Alamosa, the nearest town, for camping supplies so he could live on site while he waited for their return.

The summer started well at La Garita Ranch, but a herder had to go back to Mexico as some relative had died. This happened fairly often with our Mexican herders. It was puzzling how the very same relatives seemed to die about every three months. The loneliness of herding sheep was very hard for people as sociable as they were by nature, and it was easy to empathize with how they longed for fun, friends and probably some delicious Dos Equis beer. Off they went. Most were good men, and we liked them, so Dom let them go and welcomed them back after the "funerals."

Dom took little Paul, barely eight years old, to replace the herder. He was left alone to herd 2000 sheep just as Dom had been when he was that age. At night Paul stayed in the headquarters, a falling-apart old house with an ancient Mexican cook who kept him fed with tortillas and beans. When Dom came home without him I hit the ceiling. I had assumed Paul was with his dad all that time. My mother happened to be visiting and was just as furious. She demanded that

44

I go get him, sheep be damned, and Dom be damned. I left the family in her care and drove as fast as I dared across Colorado. My little son, scared, his dark eyes big with fear, ran to me as I drove up. His words tumbled out about how hard it had been taking care of all those sheep. He was sure if he lost any his dad would just kill him. Dom scrambled to get a new man. I was afraid he would be furious with me, but he said nothing. Paul had tales to tell his friends and bragging to do about the Spanish he had learned and how he could now make tortillas, which not even his old Ma could do. The Terrible Tempered Mr. Bang was a real hero.

Dom leased many other ranches, among them one near Bosler, where Dom, Elaine, Anne, Paul and Dave were gathering cows and calves. Dom had something important he had to get to so he left them saying, "Bring them in. Don't leave any behind!" A thunderstorm threatened; thunder, lightning and rain advanced ominously. Calves scattered in fright and they struggled to get them back with their mothers and through a gate into the next pasture. They knew that lightning could strike a fence at a distance and travel down the wires to shock the heck out of anything that touched it. That gate had to be opened, the cows and calves pushed through and the gate closed. The kids took a vote and decided to leave the cattle they had gathered and get to a cow camp and a warm fire. They had no slickers, were soaked, miserable and freezing cold and for the first time, dared to brave their Dad's wrath. Dom returned, sized up the situation and said nothing.

Next, Dom leased a ranch owned by French Basques with the

same last name as ours, but spelled in the French version. It was in the mountains east of Cokeville and had the biggest mosquitoes in the whole world. I paused in sagebrush taller than a horse and pulled down my Levis. No sooner had I squatted than millions attacked and my entire derriere was covered in the damned things! I got my pants back up as quickly as I could. I scratched my itching backside for a week. How unladylike!

La Veta Pass was high in the southern Colorado mountains, however we leased the ranch for only one summer as Grizzlies, coyotes and mountain lions decimated our sheep. It was devastating. There was also a ranch, The Baca Grant, in the mountains west of Los Alamos, New Mexico, which we rented only once because it was too far away. Our favorite places were in Wyoming. The Schwabacher ranch near Pinedale, and the Lembcke spread south of Laramie were beautiful, each in its distinctive way, and we befriended such great people, the chaos was a small price to pay. But chaos it was. No matter, we were good at "carrying on disirregardless." (That is not a proper word, but how we carried on wasn't proper either.)

Perilous Driving

The leased ranches were all different, but they all required exhausting, endless work. Dom was so overworked and stressed that he could not stay awake driving—the cause of some of his many accidents. Over the twenty-two years we were together, Dom's terrible driving resulted in sixteen crashes and multiple dashes to emergency

46

rooms. Though he often took some of the children with him, they were never involved in any of his accidents, truly a miracle. No way could the reality of guardian angels be doubted.

Driving recklessly and irresponsibly—even reading mail as he sped down the highway—got Dom arrested so many times his license was revoked twice. First, for a year and later for three years he was forbidden to drive. He hired drivers, but everyone folded under the pressure so he went back to driving himself. Of course insurance was revoked on the nine trucks that our foremen used. I actually developed knee problems from praying. Faithful friend Dr. Haley examined me with something close to horror, and said, "For God's sake, if you have to pray that much, at least do it standing up!" The Voice deep in my mind agreed, whispering, "My children are not lowly supplicants to be kneeling, eyes cast down. Pray standing up, eyes open and looking Heavenward!" So I did, and it lifted me to joy and hope.

This was a good thing, as times became scarier than ever. As soon as Paul could see over the dashboard Dom handed the wheel over to him, commanding, "Drive," so he could sleep. Paul was only seven years old. One time Dom woke up suddenly and yelled, "You missed the turn! We have to go to Lander!" Paul remembers doing a "donut," skidding in a circle, tires screeching, in the big truck right in the middle of the highway, more afraid of his Dad's fury than of any oncoming traffic. On to Lander they went. Dave was taught to drive, too, and those two little boys logged thousands of miles, long before they were old enough for licenses.

Elaine, also taught to drive when she was seven, was given a responsibility as dangerous as Dom's demand that the little boys drive him on Colorado and Wyoming freeways. She was just a young teen-ager when Dom taught her how to drive one of the big, multi-geared trucks and sent her, alone, on errands far and wide.

On one trip she was driving down a long slope on a two-track dirt road when the brakes failed. The truck gained speed terrifyingly but she couldn't gear down as the transmission had gone out too. A curve loomed ahead next to a steep ravine, and as Elaine struggled to make the turn, the steering went out! She was about to jump out to save herself when guardian angels came to the rescue. Suddenly the whole back wheel assembly dropped off the truck with a sickening roar. In the rearview mirror she saw the four double wheels careening dizzily off into the sagebrush. With horror, she thought, "What next?" The rear end ground into the dirt and dragged the truck to a stop at the edge of the ravine. Elaine, knees shaking, got out and hiked in the pouring rain about seven of the eight miles back to the ranch. Milton Newell, the county road grader, came upon her and picked her up. He took her the rest of the way in his big machine and talked about his "rescue mission" for years, obviously quite taken with young Elaine.

Anne was just learning to drive and was coming down the canyon in the station wagon when she crashed into the sage. The boys pulled the station wagon out with a truck and Anne told me, "There was a darling family of raccoons crossing the road, the mom, the dad and some babies. I had to swerve to save their lives!" Of course I believed her. Years later it seeped out that there had been no raccoons but there had been a bota of wine.

A Little Help from Our Friends—The Etchepares

Our nomadic lifestyle throughout the West introduced us to many people in the wool growing industry; ranchers, farmers, lamb and wool buyers, but the time and attention it took to build real friendships was hard to come by. Occasionally relationships developed that surpassed business and gave us lifelong friends who were supportive, encouraging and fun.

Paul Etchepare was a lamb buyer, business associate, French Basque, and friend of Dom's. He and his wife Hellen lived in a beautiful home in Denver. Hellen was a role model for me in the way she handled disaster. As in almost all families there were accidents, illnesses, and teen-age excitements. Hellen, with Paul's support, handled everything with such wisdom and graciousness that I took note, emulating her as best I could as cystic fibrosis devastated our family and excitements kept storming in upon us.

Paul embarked on an enterprise that eventually gave him ownership of Warren Livestock and the Pole Creek Ranch, and they moved from Denver to Cheyenne, Wyoming. He wanted Dom to enter into a partnership with him, but Dom wisely declined. What fireworks might have erupted between those two "Bascos" in a partnership! Our friendships were thus preserved, and merrily we often joined them in Cheyenne.

49

At one of the Etchepare soirées, the nicest man and I struck up a lively, long conversation. Later, when I told Hellen about him she said, "He is indeed charming, and he writes so well!" "Writes? He is a writer?" I asked. "Soph, he's James Michener!" No wonder he found me so amusing. How fun for someone so famous to realize I had no idea who he was.

With their many prestigious friends, Hellen and Paul put the Cystic Fibrosis Foundation on the map in both Colorado and Wyoming. Dom and I joined them, of course, and we worked hard and successfully. I was charged with running drives for the Cystic Fibrosis Foundation in our beautiful little hometown of Longmont, north of Denver. About 70% of the money raised came from small donations, many from going door to door. Only 30% was coughed up in significant chunks, so never do I turn up my nose at a five-dollar bill or a little check, and small checks are what I write to some of those heart-rending pleas we all get. No shame, as those little offerings, often given with difficulty and good heart, add up.

Those twenty years we worked for the Cystic Fibrosis Foundation were gratifying. As research yields newer and better drugs and treatments, there is hope that Cystics can live longer lives of better quality. How good it was to have been a part of making it so.

A Road Not Traveled Much

Jumping Jeepers! The tsunami of business was threatening to sink me. As Lorelei Lee (*Gentlemen Prefer Blondes*) said, "I was on the verge of standing more than I could bear." It was 1966, and there were 50,000 sheep in Colorado and Wyoming, 34 herders, the Colorado farm and the several feedlots where we had lambs. It was unlikely we would see much of old Dad, as the kids called him, for some time.

For old Ma, as they kindly called me, school loomed, clothes had to be assembled, the house put in some kind of order, and our beautiful yard rescued from weeds and detritus after our summer away chasing sheep. On top of that, I was committed to help with several Cystic Fibrosis Foundation fundraising events in Denver and Cheyenne. Most daunting was the office, my desk piled sky high with mail to be read, and a million calls to be answered. The kids scattered hither and yon to catch up with their friends and no doubt astound them with tales of their adventures. I hoped our guardian angels would keep them out of the hospital or jail.

They let us down on the hospital, and both Pete and Joseph went in for clean outs, their lungs filled with the unspeakable gunk that so plagues, and eventually kills kids with cystic fibrosis. (One time a doctor asked Joseph what color the stuff he was coughing up was. I had bought a fancy gift for a fancy friend at very fancy Gucci's, and the green Gucci shopping bag was sitting on a chair. Joseph looked over at it and said, "Gucci green," a term that left the doctor scratching his head.) Meanwhile, Dom was so hurried and harried that he lost a $23,000 check. He sent me to Swift & Co., (who had issued it for a ship-ment of fat lambs) to stop payment and to get another. Good heavens, no wonder he sent me. Hardly anyone loses checks like that, and he

51

assumed I could bear the shame better than he could. Then he did it again, this time a check for $21,000. Not even I was that haphazardly out of control! I went about getting payment stopped and a new check issued wondering what was going on with Dom.

Dom came home, took one look at my desk covered with stacks of paper and asked, "Where are the kids?" "How the heck would I know?" was my frustrated reply. I had faith in their survival skills and was not worried about their safety, though the safety of the neighborhood wasn't such a sure thing. Dom realized something must be done, and he hired help. Heaven surely had something to do with how he found Monica Barela.

Nice ladies would not come to baby-sit or clean because there were always Basque foremen and herders, rough looking men, living in our basement and eating with us. Monica Barela spoke Spanish and was one powerful old gal. She kept the men right in line and did pretty well with the children, too. She looked like a true bruja (witch); short, wiry and wily, a long, sharp nose, black eyes flashing mischief and an unruly mane of salt and pepper hair. Superstitious and spiritual in the intense way Mexicans often are, there was no doubt she could cast spells and impose curses, but I was sure she was really an angel. Men, cats, dogs, and children were her slaves. She even cracked the whip over me and taught me useful skills I would never learn from nice ladies and certainly not from my mother.

Our horrible neighbor, Mrs. Seewald, railed at Dom about all the dandelions in our lawn—they were blowing seeds into hers. Dom took her side and railed at me, "My mother always pulled the dandelions out. What's wrong with you?" Monica sped to my rescue and taught me how to make dandelion wine. She also showed me how to administer honey and brandy when someone was sick. It would cure anything, or at least make the patient not care so much about recovery. I somehow missed the fact that she also taught the children how to brew corn whiskey.

With Monica's help, life came close enough to being in control that Dom could leave to take care of our livelihood, our beloved sheep. He needed pasture, lots of it, and he took off on a major search.

Dom headed north to check out three ranches, Echo Springs, Sourdough and Siberia Ridge, about forty miles west of Rawlins, near the little town of Wamsutter. They were spread across high desert, as the swath of land that swept across the middle and southern part of Wyoming was called. Scant rain and snowfall rendered it semi-desert and at 6,000 feet, it qualified as high. Still lower than the surrounding high mountains, it afforded a climate that was, for Wyoming, relatively mild. It provided excellent range for fall, summer, and spring grazing, though winters there were too brutal to sustain livestock operations that were profitable.

The land would not impress anyone but livestock people. As far as the eye could see there was nothing but hardy Indian wheat grass dotted with outcroppings of sagebrush and a few low hills. Two areas of badlands lay near the southern border of Echo Springs Ranch, their steep hills, deep canyons, caves and cliffs of naked dirt looking otherworldly. In the middle of approximately 100,000 acres, the springs for which the ranch was named bubbled up. The water was loaded with minerals rendering them barely drinkable by livestock and wildly laxative for any cowboy thirsty enough to try it. Other sources of water were good, rain collected in ponds, or tanks as they were called, scattered around the ranches. Next to one stood the only tree on the entire place, a brave little cottonwood.

Antelope traversed the two ranches, Siberia Ridge and Sourdough, to the north of Wamsutter. They were gathering places for their herds in the fall, and two to three thousand streaked across the sage, congregating for mating and their winter migrations. Dom had been lucky enough to be there one autumn, and the beauty of their race thrilled him. Across the wide land, their white rumps bobbing up and down, their smooth, tan backs rolling like ocean waves, they ran, in a rare, wild, and wondrous celebration of life.

McCarty Canyon Ranch, high in the foothills of the Sierra Madre Range was about fifty miles to the east of Echo Springs and served as headquarters for the four ranches. It was well known as one of the best areas in Wyoming, as it stayed green all summer, unlike most of Wyoming that saw grass go brown in July. The hay it produced was excellent and the buildings, the fences and corrals were good. Best of all it had plenty of good water. The owners of the four properties had always lived there, as it was the only place that had buildings. Consequently McCarty Canyon Ranch was never available for lease, but Dom knew about it. Everyone knew about McCarty Canyon Ranch. Dom wondered if there was a chance that he could lease any of those beautiful places. He managed a summer on Echo Springs, where our band of breeding rams thrived, but the rest of the properties remained out of reach—until fate intervened.

Oh! Spectacular Fate

The Artie Rasmussen family had homesteaded McCarty Canyon and the three desert ranches back in the 1800's. Artie and Edna grew too old and frail to take care of their properties and as painful as it must have been, they found it necessary to sell them in 1962. Along came the Bannings, rich enough to snap them up quickly, making it possible for the two old pioneers to move to Rawlins where they could retire comfortably.

Roger Banning, handsome and distinguished, owned large enterprises in New York. He and his elegant wife had two young adult sons who had begun to veer away from accepted behavior, to put it politely. Roger had traveled in Wyoming and loved the isolation and beauty. "A ranch there might be the very thing to straighten my boys out," he thought. By happy chance he found the Rasmussen ranches forty miles from Rawlins, remote enough to keep the boys out of trouble. Roger flew to the McCarty Ranch, landing on a stretch of road near the headquarters that was long and smooth enough for his small plane. The two sons followed in their sports car and launched, maybe lurched, enthusiastically into becoming cowboys. Mrs. Banning flew in only once, but she was an aloof New Yorker,

55

preferring her city to wild Wyoming, so she left, never to return.

The McCarty ranch house was a rustic two-room log cabin nearly a hundred years old. A large log kitchen had been tacked on. A cranky old generator supplied electricity and plumbing was minimal. Entirely different from their big New York home, it was with apprehension Roger and his sons moved in. They had not heard the saying, "Wyoming is not for sissies," nor had it occurred to them that running a ranch would be different from what they had seen on TV and in the movies. They floundered about in confusion and frustration. It wasn't long before Roger's hopes for his sons began to fade.

The boys wrecked their snazzy sports car racing over the rocky two-track dirt road after partying in Rawlins, most likely schnockered. It was a wonder they survived. Their cattle did not thrive; the hay meadows withered away, and the lovely gardens Artie and Edna had planted around the house died. The place was going downhill and the boys were wilder than ever.

The coup de grâs came one day when Mrs. Banning called from New York. Roger was staying at the Ferris Hotel, Rawlins's finest, and she asked to be connected to Mr. Banning's room. The girl on the hotel switchboard cheerfully chirped, "Oh, he and his wife just walked out the door!" Apparently Roger was a little wild himself.

Mrs. Banning called her attorneys. Roger went to Mexico, and the boys returned to New York where they belonged. The ranches were put up for auction in 1967. Precipitously.

News of the dramatic exodus and the resulting auction got to

Dom. The sale was so distressed the ranches might sell way below market and he wanted to be ready to pounce on them. He quickly got Prudential Insurance Company to finance him, quite an accomplishment, and he was set to go. His plan was such a closely guarded secret that none of us, not even I, knew a thing.

Dom chose David, ten years old, to go with him to Casper where the auction was to be held. There was no time to drive, so a little plane was chartered and, rocking and rolling, they took off for Wyoming. The big event was to take place in a hotel conference room and Dom found two seats in the middle where they could see all that went on but hardly be noticed. It would be an advantage if no one could see he was bidding.

The auctioneer pounded his gavel and the sale began. Dave said he did not know his Dad intended to bid, but before long he noticed that every time Dom touched the brim of his hat, the bidding changed. The very neighbors Artie Rasmussen had hoped would be able to buy his beloved home before Roger Banning stepped in were in hot competition, determined not to let those ranches get away from them again. The bidding grew hot and contentious. No one noticed Dom. He never stirred. He just kept putting finger to hat brim.

There was only one short break in the long, tense day and everyone exited. Dave escaped to the hotel restaurant with Sam, their young pilot, for life saving hamburgers. Back in their seats, he watched as his dad again sat dead still, moving only that finger to his hat brim. Suddenly the auctioneer slammed his gavel down and announced loudly, "Echo Springs, Siberia Ridge, Sour Dough and McCarty Canyon Ranches are sold to Dr. Echeverria!" Dave was blown-away-astonished and Dom was quietly triumphant. A new life was about to begin.

The flight back was joyous until the little plane lost power and began to flounder. The pilot, Sam, did not want to scare young Dave, so he made a game of finding unlikely landing places saying, "Look for fields where our little plane could land!" Dave peered out one side, Dom the other, searching as late afternoon cast long deceptive shadows, yelling, "There's a corn field!" or, "How about that stretch of highway?" The little plane sputtered and shook, but Sam kept urging it on hoping for somewhere, anywhere, to land. Dave said they were too busy looking for suitable places, and Sam kept making it a game, so he was not as terrified as he should have been. The radio had quit, so Sam signaled their distress by dipping his wings and someone got the message. Dave wondered about the fire engines that were suddenly speeding along below them as they approached a little field near Boulder, Colorado. They slid shuddering to safety, the fire engines racing to their aid.

I was at the University of Colorado Medical Center in Denver, where I had spent the day doing what I could to cheer Pete on in his courageous fight to survive. Night fell, Pete was ready for sleep. I left for the forty-mile drive home to Longmont. To get my mind off the hospital I switched on a Denver news station just in time to hear, "Dr. Domingo Echeverria of Longmont bought four ranches today at an auction in Casper. They are located in Carbon and Sweetwater counties in south central Wyoming in the Rawlins area and comprise over 100,000 acres."

WHAT? Holy Moses! I nearly fell off the freeway and then I got a speeding ticket. Our world was exploding! Great change was about to happen.

Top: Dom Echeverria's family trailing their sheep up the Hassayampa River on a two-week trip to Cross Mountain Ranch, circa 1920. Left: Dr. Dom Echeverria's dark good looks hid an equally dark, sometimes cruel, side of his personality. This photo was taken in 1969, less than a year from his unexpected death.

Top: The teenaged author, before she met Dom, holding her beloved dog Linda. One of the great sadnesses of her life would be Dom's lack of empathy and connection to dogs that were not working ranch animals, an odd characteristic that resulted in him shooting several family pets—occasionally in front of their children.

Top and bottom, respectively: The author and Dom at Cross Mountain Ranch, an historic Echeverria family property in Northern Arizona. The author recounts that she feared her family would drown when crossing one of the creeks on the ranch during a "frog strangler." Despite inherent dangers, she realized early on that she was drawn to ranching as a way of life to raise her own family.

Opposite page, top: Hundreds of sheep descend a hillside on a ranch near Parshall, Colorado, to reach water. Dom leased the livestock ranch—also the home of the famed Buckhorn guest ranch—in 1964. Bottom: Dom riding with sons Pete, foreground, and younger son Paul. Dom struggled with challenges posed by Pete's cystic fibrosis, creating an oft times strained relationship between himself and his son. Photo circa 1962.

This page, above: Pete is all smiles as he helps corral lambs, circa 1965. Opposite page, top: Joseph displays a big grin en route to La Garita Ranch in Colorado, 1964. Joseph was one of three Echeverria children born with cystic fibrosis. Bottom: Paul, age 8, works sheep in a corral, 1964.

Top: Joseph, age 5, and beloved dog Mayi herd sheep in Wyoming, 1967. Right: At age 3, Joseph skillfully braces himself in the back of a ranch pick-up truck—and relishes the ride.

Top: Joseph, Anne, Paul, Sophie, Dave and Pete explore red rock formations on the Lembcke Ranch, one of many properties leased by Dom. Left: Anne and Pete en route to Lembcke's. Note the sheep inside the car.

Top: "A few little woolies" find company in a Wyoming corral. Bottom: Elaine, Paul, Dave, Joseph, Sophie, Anne and herder Julian Muguiro stake out a high perch on large wool bags.

Top: Big Enough, Barak and Joseph ride in the pick-up bed as we move out of camp. Bottom: Camping in the Wyoming Wagon on our Tosi forest permit. Gorgeous, spectacular country.

Top: Unloading sheep on Echo Springs Ranch. Full-size semis transported thousands of woolies to our fall pasture. Bottom: Julian Muguiro, a Basque from Spain who was so much a part of our lives.

70

McCarty Canyon Ranch:
Home of Our Hearts

School at last was out, and we could leave Longmont for Wyoming. It was 1967. Excitedly I packed the station wagon, loaded seven children, two dogs, and several cats and we took off. Dom, already there, gave typical Wyoming directions, "You go south out of Rawlins towards some mountains that have pine groves on them. Go up Miller Hill, no signs, but you can't miss it—it is a hill, for gosh sakes, go past some corrals and then take the road to the right. Watch it where the road crosses the pond—slick, you could fall in." I packed plenty of survival food and water in case of disaster.

The country was magnificent. As we reached the top of Miller Hill the view seemed to take in all of Wyoming, wide open and free as the wind. "It feels like we really belong here!" one of the children exclaimed. "It is the home of our souls!" another added. Then on we drove to the slick slide near the pond. "Whoa!" we all yelled as we slid almost into the water. The kids shouted, "Step on the gas!" and we made it out splattering mud far and wide. Another long slippery slope, newly soaked in rain, challenged us as we slid around just missing a drop into a deep draw on one side and a rocky bank on the other. And then we topped out. We had arrived at the cattle guard that marked the boundary of McCarty Canyon Ranch.

To the south we could see the mountains, still capped with snow, around Steamboat Springs near the Colorado state line some fifty miles away. More mountains and the dark, ominous Rattlesnake Butte, an ancient volcanic extrusion, rose in the distance. It seemed we could see forever. We were home and we knew it. We felt it in our very bones.

The road sloped down along the canyon floor. Patches of thick sagebrush bordered lush, green meadows. Sage chickens fluttered out squawking and flapping as we approached, taking cover in the aspen and pine groves on the hillsides. The ranch sat on the continental divide, a geological blessing that caused all the water on the place to be born in springs. We stopped and hiked to one where water bubbled up through sand, clear and clean, to form a lovely stream. There were fish, and frogs, and watercress. Flowers bloomed everywhere and the air smelled bracingly fresh, flower fragrance and the gentle pungency of sage mixed in a celebration of spring. The trails elk and deer made as they came down out of the forests to water beckoned to us. They surely led to magical places and we longed to explore, but first, onward to the ranch headquarters.

Suddenly around a bend, there was our home. A large barn loomed up surrounded by corrals and fenced pastures where horses and sheep grazed. To the right was a log cabin sheltered beneath a grand cottonwood tree. Honeysuckle vines so old they had climbed the yard's fence to form a fragrant wall of greenery. A garage, coal house, chicken house, a little cabin and two outhouses surrounded the main log home. Willows and flowers festooned the stream banks. Wild ducks cruised peacefully on the clear water, "bottoming up" as they dove for food. Beavers had built dams just downstream forming large ponds. We pulled up and piled out. Dom was waiting for us and our greetings were uproarious. Our great adventure had begun.

We rolled up our sleeves and dove into cleaning the houses. The Banning boys were really slobs and had left so suddenly that we were faced with quite a mess. It seemed as though in the five years they had lived there they had never washed their sheets or towels. Brown and smelly, we dumped them in a washing machine run by a gasoline lawn mower motor. Dom found it in Rawlins and bought it as a welcoming gift for me. A roller wringer topped it, and we cranked the sheets and everything else through by hand, to be rinsed in an ancient bathtub. By golly, it got them sort of clean. The fresh air and bright sunshine finished the job as we hung them out on the clotheslines. They would be forever beige but they smelled good.

A wood cook stove, resplendent with chrome and blue enamel, stood at the end of the kitchen. We fired it up, which took so much effort we cooked everything we could think of while it was hot; biscuits, stews, beans, and Basque rice pudding bubbled and simmered. The long kitchen table became the scene of fine feasts.

Sheep were delivered to the ranch in big triple-decked semi-trucks. The road was a challenge and it took real nerve and skill to negotiate the trip. All of us, especially the sheep, were greatly relieved when they pulled into the ranch to be unloaded. The children, small and quick, scurried into the trucks' three decks to shoo the sheep out. Chispas, Buddy and Olivia, good sheep dogs, snapped at their heels and got them moving. Our very little dog, Mayi, a black and tan mutt, was the most effective, as the sheep did not know what to make of her. Was she a dog, or what? Her little yips really worked and ewes and lambs streamed out, bleating loudly as they searched for each other. Soon bands were formed, averaging between twelve hundred and two thousand. They streamed onto the meadows eager for good grass, their herders following.

The truckers were greeted with admiration and gratitude for getting our sheep home safely, and we fed them well. We also entertained wool buyers, lamb buyers, and anyone else who drifted in. It was Wyoming custom, cast in granite that anyone who nears a ranch must be invited in. Usually there were at least a dozen people at our table, counting the children and the herders, and sometimes the long table was set for as many as twenty-four.

Mutton was the main entree. If any poor critter looked as though it might die, someone shot it, dressed it out and brought it in for me to cut up and cook. Dom saw to it that none of the meat was dangerously diseased. Sometimes we had poached game when Dom shot antelope from his pickup window going forty miles an hour. When game ran, adrenalin pumped into their systems and produced

74

bad tasting meat, so he learned to take them down before they even saw him. I was never able to overcome my horror and sorrow when animals were killed, though I tried to be brave about it and I had to admire Dom's skill.

Sage chickens were plentiful and delicious. The boys hunted them for special occasions and the girls and I fired up the wood stove and roasted them. They were moist and tender with a subtle natural sage flavor. We served them with pride, except the time I tried to be really creative and made a stuffing of fresh Wyoming sage. Good God, it tasted like the soap my mother used to make out of lye and tallow. (I knew how it tasted as Mom washed my mouth out with it for swearing.)

Doing dishes for such crowds was a challenge. Elaine, beautiful and efficient, was chief of the operation. One of the Basques Dom had imported from Spain, Julian Muguiro, was so handsome his picture appeared in several Western publications. He had a mad crush on Elaine. How fortunate! There he was hauling stacks of dishes, towel at the ready, and as close to her as he could get. With Anne and little Sophie they made up quite a crew.

The dishes were washed in a funky old sink with water pumped from the stream, but we realized early that it was not for drinking. A dead sheep was found floating in it and beavers, birds, and unknown critters with no idea of sanitation were sharing it. We hoped it was safe for the dishes. A spring that sprang out of a bank near the barn supplied clean water for table use, and it also served as our "refrigerator," keeping food somewhat cool.

We believed we were doing just fine, but were we? It came back to us through the grapevine that if you visited the Echeverrias in Wyoming, you would be well advised to take your own food. Longmont friends felt they narrowly escaped a horrible end in our "unconventional" kitchen. Many of them regarded a visit as "interesting" though perilous, and they came with coolers of their own, safe food. We had to agree that scraping maggots out of rotting ham and occasionally running out of food was not sufficiently civilized. Driving forty miles over the terrible road to Rawlins was often out of the question, so we did creative things with canned string beans and made pies out of the rhubarb that survived under the clothesline. The watercress, from what our friends saw as polluted streams, didn't quite do it for them either, but we loved it.

The bathroom had a toilet that did not work, a sink good enough to brush teeth in and an old fashioned tub that stood on four lion paw legs where we rinsed the laundry. A propane-fired water heater that started with a terrifying BOOM produced enough hot water for the washing machine and showers. The room badly needed decorating. We found curtains in Rawlins for the big window that cheered it up some, but the long bare wall next to the sink needed a poster. I had seen one in a shop in Larimer Square, a chichi-hippie area in Denver, that would have been perfect but it was not for sale. It pictured a lady of the 1800's perched on one of those tricycles popular then, with a front wheel almost as tall as she was and two small wheels behind. She wore stylish laced boots, a glorious flower-bedecked hat and nothing else. I painted my version of the poster half life-sized, really quite good, on the wall. The truckers, the lamb and wool buyers and most everyone else liked it. It added a touch of class to the ratty old bathroom.

The outhouse needed some sprucing up, too. We painted it white on the inside and then wrote wise and funny sayings with Marks-a-Lot all over it. It became a kind of intellectual Mecca, and guests added their bons mots. Unfortunately some guests were not up to our intellectual standards and they wrote witless, icky stuff that we had to paint over. What was it with some people that they needed to degrade a place as elegant as our outhouse?

Dom and I had the end room. The bed was placed so I could look out the window at the cottonwood tree with its joyfully chattering bird colonies. At night stars sparkled through the branches making it seem a magical Christmas tree. Beyond, the high ridges rose, spotted here and there with grazing sheep, cattle and horses. I was so in love with it I cranked out this little poem:

> Silence singing a night song,
> Yes, silence sings if you simply
> Be still and listen.
> A quiet so deep it is Holy,
> Revealing another reality.
> A smell soft and sweet---alive!
> Meadow grass and sage sighing fragrance.

Stars shining through leaves of the
Sacred Rustling Tree.
Our souls dancing in this universe,
Clothed in grey mists of night cloud,
Iridescent, spangled with stars.
The moon casting its silver spell,
Lending enchantment and magic to
Hills and meadows,
Quite as lovely as the daytime
Sunshine embrace.

Elaine, Sophie, and Anne took the cabin across the lawn. At first they called their little home the TV Rooms because the herders peeked through the windows to watch the girl show. A raunchy, ugly Spaniard, Jose, used to look in and whisper menacingly to Anne, "Good morning, little girl." He had molested her back in Longmont, (unknown to me,) and Dom nevertheless allowed him to be on the ranch with our children. He was a good herder and Dom liked him. Despite my fear of his retaliation I fought Dom to get rid of him and finally he was gone. Did he take him to the feedlot (ie. kill him), or send him back to Spain? Whichever, thank God we never saw him again, but the sad realization that Dom would not protect us lingered. Essentially on our own, we devised ways to keep us safe. We managed to get the generator to generate just long enough to power our sewing machine so we could make curtains to protect the little ladies. They found rugs and hung pictures to make their home comfortably pretty and relatively secure.

The old generator held on long enough for us to make drapes for the living room. I found some gorgeous designer fabric in Denver, and I bought it, expense be damned. Dramatic black, strewn with a glorious profusion of flowers, they made our living room lovely. Couches, chairs, a coffee table, Navajo rugs, a few paintings and our bookcase made the place comfortable and charming, the kids and I thought. Dom was not so sure it was all that lovely and said, "It would be a good thing if it just burned down and we got a house trailer." Holy denigration! We would be trailer park trash! Whatever was he thinking?

Joseph, Dave, Paul, Pete and cousin Roy rotated around between the room next to the living room and the bunkroom off the kitchen. Their decorations were confined to gun racks and old magazines. I found some Playboys under their beds. Dom responded to my pleas of "DO something!" with, "So, what?" Hmmmm—"So what" indeed. Powerless was what I was.

At a gas station in Laramie there was a rack that had a Playgirl magazine. "AHA," I thought. "I'll just get even with those boys," so I bought it. Holy amazing projections! I never dreamed... The boys laughed their heads off at their old Ma, and the girls snatched the darned thing away never to be found again. Oh well.

The rats and mice that lived so happily with us ate the generator wiring and it died. We segued to candles, which were lovely, and Coleman and kerosene lanterns. With no electricity, there was no radio and no TV. We played cards and read, went to bed when darkness fell and got up with the sun.

One morning as we fired up the wood cook stove, Elaine grabbed what she thought was the kerosene can to stoke it, but it was the highly volatile white gas for the Coleman lanterns. She sloshed some on the kindling wood and the place burst into flames. By the grace of God all she suffered was singed eyebrows and bangs. With a terrified yell she slung the can across the room spewing gas as it went and the place was an inferno in seconds. Our pet deer, Pilareen, had never seen fire and she stood transfixed. Joseph grabbed her and got her to safety. I dashed around yelling, "Throw the books out the windows!" Our books were our most prized possessions. We sped around gathering Navajo rugs and pictures saving what we could.

Dom, Pete, Paul, Anne, and Dave were riding up on Buffalo Ridge, driving cattle down to the corrals. They could see the ranch house from there, and Paul yelled, "What the hell? Mom is throwing books out the front door!" "Oh my God, the house is on fire! We better get down there fast!" Dave hollered. Dom commanded, "Keep the cattle together! We have to get them moved first and there isn't anything we can do anyway. Mom can take care of it just fine." He was confident I wouldn't let anyone burn up in it and was probably relishing thoughts of house trailers. Cousin Roy found a fire extinguisher and put the whole thing out, a hero for at least that day.

The next week was spent scrubbing soot off everything. Dom loaned us Andres Irustia, one of the herders. Andres was an interesting character. During World War II he had joined the infamous Spanish Blue Division, which joined the Nazis to fight the Russians. The Basques violently opposed communism because it was so virulently against the Catholic Church and God Himself. They believed it was their holy duty to fight Russia no matter how they did it. Eventually they were dissuaded from their collusion with the Nazis and they left for home. The little, burley, funny looking man had a history. Now here he was, an outlaw, wanted by the Spanish Policia for involvement with the Nazis and with ETA, the Basque terrorist group.

He got up on the long kitchen table with bucket and mop at the ready and washed the whole smoke-smudged ceiling. The lovely sky-blue paint we had just put on reemerged. Meanwhile, we were scrubbing walls, counters, and floors with all our might while we struggled not to embarrass Andres with our barely suppressed laughter. As he swabbed the ceiling, he sang little Basque songs and farted thunderously almost in time to his music. Never had we been so "exquisitely entertained"! Our ribs hurt from trying not to laugh.

We had a phone for the first few years on McCarty Canyon Ranch, a party line, with a single wire that served our neighbors, Buzz and Betsy Rendle on their Grizzly Ranch, and us. (Buzz was so named because as a Colonel in the Air Force he used to buzz Rawlins in his fighter plane.) The phone died and no one could fix it though Lord knows we tried. Buzz drove up and commandeered the boys to help, and on Dom's orders, off they went, but it was futile. No one who knew how to fix it would come out the forty miles from Rawlins. We owned it, the longest private line ever, so the public phone company was no help. There we were, phoneless, which we discovered was very nice.

My mother, the unique and marvelous Sophie Burden, now called Granny Soph, came to visit. One dark night the dead phone line began to hum loudly. At the same time northern lights, gorgeously iridescent green and gold began to dance in the sky over Buffalo Ridge north of the house. Granny Soph was awakened, no doubt by the mystic voices with which she was blessed, and she dashed out into the yard, her nightie flapping in the breeze. "They are coming! The UFO's are about to land! Fire up the stove and get out the tea pot so we can welcome them!" Darn, they stood us up, but it was a hilarious night and while we laughed, we were also swept away with the beauty of it. There was never any doubt that The Force, Yahweh, God, Whoever, was swirling all around.

A strange thing happens in the silence of Wyoming, elsewhere too, but McCarty Canyon was where we experienced it. At first I thought with alarm that something was wrong with my ears or my brain. Then others in the family described it too. There was a hum, a really mystical kind of hum. The old phone line that had hummed with the Northern Lights had been taken out so it was not that. I felt immersed in something otherworldly and transcendent as I listened in the star-studded night. Holy? Absolutely! Later, as I explored esoteric persuasions, I read that the hum was the Sound of the Universe, the grand Om, and that we were extraordinarily blessed to have heard it.

Who were we, anyway? Such exquisiteness embraced us, such

joyous spirituality, and yet violence, heartbreak, tragedy, and shockingly destructive behavior dogged us. Miraculously we always seemed
able to cope. Hey, God, Krishna, Brahma, Yahweh, The Force, thanks a
bunch! "All is well, all is very well," to quote Voltaire's Candide.

Neighbors, Some of Them Ghosts

Not long after we moved in, the boys climbed up into the attic
and found a stash of embalming fluid and strange instruments. Who
had been an undertaker, and whom had they undertaken, those many
years ago? We searched for burial sites but found nothing but prairie
dog mounds and critter bones. The dead cowboys, miners, sheepherders, or lost souls who were dragged into McCarty Canyon must have
been carted away after they were embalmed.

Their ghosts remained, haunting us in the dark quiet nights.
Anne, especially, could sense them. An artist and a writer, she was ex-
tra sensitive, so "Anna Banana" as we lovingly titled her, was a prime
target for restless spirits. They whooshed and rustled about, scaring
her half to death until she eventually became used to them.

Petroglyphs on the Lembcke Ranch unveiled ghosts of a different sort. A few years before Dom bought our ranches, and for a
time afterwards, he leased a place south of Laramie that promised not
only good grazing, but also fun for the children. Lush with fields of
fine pasture, it was transected by a range of picturesque, towering red
rocks. The secret canyons and caves begged for exploration, and the
cliffs of course had to be scaled. Dave yelled, "Hey, come look at this!"

He had discovered petroglyphs carved in a red sandstone wall that whispered of a past peopled by Indians.

There were several drawings carved in the rock that depicted what must have been space men. They pictured helmets and suits that were unlike any of the other drawings. Rock art of what looked like aliens had been found in many areas throughout the west where natives live, and those of us happily free enough of conventional logic believed extraterrestrials had indeed visited. We listened for their ghosts and wished we could read what they had carved, but it remained a mystery. Holy disillusion and deception! We discovered that Pete, a real artist, had secretly carved the petroglyphs that Dave found! We wondered why he had been snickering slyly about those carvings.

Dom liked to nap in the soft, pink sands in the shade of the red walls while the kids explored and played and I prepared our picnics. Of course there was work to be done. Two bands of ewes and lambs had to be kept on the land designated for our use and herded daily to prevent over grazing.

Otto Lembcke, the ranch owner, was something of a tyrant, an old-country German. He admired Dom and the two spent a lot of time in the ranch home yattering away. Mrs. Lembcke, a brisk little hausfrau, invited me in once, only once, in the years we leased their pasture. Their home was Germanically perfect, as was her award-winning garden. She ordered the children away saying they must not even step on her gorgeous lawn as they might make footprints and I

84

was to enforce her dictates. Dom learned that she had been a matron at a Nazi Youth Camp during World War II, which was easy to believe. The children and I played in their hay barn and were happy not to have to put up with her. A strange little bit of evil seems to stick to Nazis, even in our Wild West.

From the darkness of Nazism, we bounced to the bright light of sheep man Doc Fulton. A ranch near the Wyoming-Colorado border that Dom also leased, around 1978, was owned by Doc and the rich widow he married. Not long after we met him, the romance imploded, and Dom helped him through his escape from her and the loss of his part ownership. Strange how rich widow romances so often crash and burn. With Dom's help, Doc retained the management and control of the ranch while the widow went off to play golf.

He was called Doc even though he had no medical schooling, because he could heal sick or wounded animals (almost as well as Dom). He loved sheep, and there was no doubt those two would be friends forever. Dom was dark and handsome, Doc was ruggedly grizzled and it was wonderful to watch them, so different yet so close, leaning on some fence talking about livestock, women and the problems they caused, laughing together.

An old-timer, Doc had worked on many places and he knew everyone in Carbon County, all the ranches, and plenty of history. We asked him about the embalming equipment, and though he didn't have an answer for that, he knew plenty about Butch Cassidy and the Sundance Kid. They had ridden into the ranch and taken over the cabin and the barn when they needed to hide out. The old homesteaders put up with them happily enough as they brought whiskey and news of the outside world. The McCarty brothers were part of the infamous Wild Bunch and had drifted in and out, using the ranch as a hideout. The Canyon was named after them.

Doc also told of how someone's wife had come down with appendicitis there in the dead of winter. Unable to get her out, her husband got his horse out of the barn, saddled him and rode up to the high ridges where the wind had blown enough snow off so they could make it to Rawlins. No doctor would ride the forty miles back with him, and when he got home, she had died.

Doc told us there was no evidence that Indians did more than pass through on hunting trips, because Wyoming winters were too harsh for them. Smart people that they were, they moved south when the Wyoming wind began to howl. We sat enthralled, listening to his stories, to his good Wyoming wisdom, and to his valuable knowledge of the country and everyone in it. The kids and I grew to rely on him as a supportive friend.

It was quite a surprise when Doc drove out to warn us that some neighboring ladies (neighboring covered about a hundred square miles) were coming to pay Mrs. Echeverria a "welcoming" call. Rumors had wafted to us that consternation arose in Carbon County when Dom bought the ranches. An outsider, indeed a foreigner born in Spain, and now living in Colorado, which to Rawlins folks was quite far away, had somehow snatched those good ranches away from the Wyoming natives. Not only that; he was married to a "dizzy blonde" who had been raised in Arizona even farther away, and they had a passel of rather undisciplined children. We did not have time to worry about it.

Cousin Roy, Pete's age, had been sent to live with us in the hope his questionable behavior would improve. (Good heavens, how could his parents be so optimistic!) He had guinea pigs he died pink and green. They lived in a kind of wire corral in the room next to the living room where the boys slept.

Paul, Pete and Dave found a young injured hawk flopping pitifully in the sagebrush. They chased him down, wrapped him in a burlap feed sack and brought him to the house to recover. He took over the top of the bookcase in the boys' room and perched there, staring at the guinea pigs below. His beady eyes also latched on to the mice that scurried across the logs and sometimes across us as we slept, never adequately kept in check by the busy cats. Every morning the kitchen had to be wiped down, covered as it was with their little tweedles, and we wondered if we were in danger of catching something. We never did. The hawk gawked. The little pigs were oblivious. The dogs wandered through quite sure they were above it all. It was a friendly place.

"My goodness gracious me!" I thought, "Wyoming hospitality is kicking in and maybe we are about to make friends." It crossed my mind that they might have heard about the naked lady on the tricycle and curiosity prompted their visit. The kids and I scurried about and had the old place spiffed up as much as an old place like that could possibly be. I even spiffed me up in my best Levis and shirt.

We cooked goodies. We were ready, and here they came.

Greetings and introductions went nicely, and we sat down in the living room for gracious conversation. Betsy Rendle was there, our nifty neighbor who belonged to the ultra-exclusive Old Baldy Club in Saratoga and played golf there almost daily. We marveled at her. It was thirty-eight miles over a dreadful road, but there she went, past our barn going fifty miles an hour in her big Cadillac, catching air as she crossed the cattle guard. It was quite a compliment that she passed up golf to welcome us. Merle and Signe Stratton came along with several other nice ladies. The girls and I served tea and cake, and all was going delightfully.

Suddenly shrieks from the boys' room split the air! Their door flew open! Out flew the hawk the boys had rescued with one of cousin Roy's pink and green guinea pigs clutched in his talons! Over the heads of the ladies, our hawk flapped and screeched, feathers flying everywhere, the little pig squirming and squealing with kids in frantic pursuit. Into the kitchen they churned like a tornado, and out the back pantry door the hawk and his lunch flew, never to be seen again. The kids stood in despair. Tears were shed.

The ladies, flustered, bustled around gathering their belongings, saying what they hoped was somehow appropriate, and off they scuttled. "Well," I thought, "At least no one else has ever held a tea party like that." Still not quite acceptable in beautiful downtown Rawlins, we went back to merrily living our merry lives.

Several years later I was settling up an account with a fencing contractor and a neighboring rancher about a fence we had in common. We scratched around, figuring and discussing, until we all agreed and paid our shares. The rancher offered me a cigarette. I said, "Thanks, I don't smoke." He drew himself up and declared, "Soph, I bet if yew smoked, yew would roll yer own!" My heart leaped for joy. I had at last achieved some kind of recognition in Carbon County society. But what? Hoping to enhance my reputation, whatever it was, I took up cigars briefly but I never inhaled.

Whiskey, Bullets and the Black Cloud

About a half-mile from the ranch house, up Dude Canyon, the kids had a hideout in an aspen grove. Just like my brothers and I when we were kids on our Remuda Ranch, they played Robin Hood. Swords were fashioned out of scrap lumber, and capes made of borrowed towels were safety pinned around their necks. What heroic deeds they must have created! One day, rain began pouring down, beating loud music on the metal roof. They put on their slickers, their cowboy hats and boots, and scurried out the door to rescue their best treasures. I went back to the office where there was a ton of business that demanded attention. After quite a long time I realized I had better check to see if they had made it home safely.

The ranch house was long and rambling, the kitchen at the opposite end from the office. Toward the middle of the place, my nose began to pick up a delectable smell wafting from somewhere. My eyes popped when I came through the kitchen door. Whoa! There on the roaring wood stove stood pots, boiling and bubbling noisily. Hoses came out of each, strung into gallon jugs on the floor into which a fragrant, golden liquid poured. My God! It was a still! My dear little children were brewing corn whiskey. That is what they had been so intent on rescuing. Robin Hood's still. Monica Barela, our sainted babysitter, had taught them how to brew corn whiskey.

Dom stormed in and said, "Good God, ranchers have died drinking home brew! He grabbed the corn from which the heavenly elixir had been made and threw it out the back door. The chickens came running! They thought they had died and gone to heaven, pecking away as fast as they could at that corn, clucking excitedly, probably saying something like, "Hey Mabel, get a load of this!" After a while the clucking kind of slowed down. They began staggering around, wings flapping haphazardly. They were schnockered out of their chicken minds! We laughed so hard our sides hurt! Would their eggs next morning be especially gourmet, laced with a delicious flavor of home brew? Alas, they were the same as always. The chickens were only a little hung over. The kids had managed to hide several jugs from their dad, which they stashed behind the living room couch.

Dom left to take care of business elsewhere. We were playing cards a few nights later, and the thought arose that we should sample the hidden brew, as Pete had. He had gotten himself deliriously, happily drunk soon after the brewing. Suddenly from behind the couch there was a BOOM, whiskey shooting almost to the ceiling! Leaping lizards! How had Pete survived? Sadly, we threw it out.

In wild Wyoming, moonshine wasn't the only threat to the children's safety. All ranchers have to be able to shoot, and Dom began teaching the children when they were no more than six years old. He bought pistols, rifles and plenty of ammunition, and lessons began. During one session, I walked a little way from the group to get something out of the truck, and a bullet zinged past my head so close I freaked out. "You crazy SOB, what in hell are you thinking, letting the kids fire so close to the truck and to me?" When I am terrified or furious, I can't help slipping back into the swearing I learned back in our ranch corrals. Sometimes, things are so bad that only a rip-snorting four-letter word will do. Gun safety? There must have been some instruction about it, as no one in our family has been shot, and in fact, both Paul and Dave became National Rifle Association Gold Medalist Sharp Shooters.

Eventually there were bullet holes in not only the ranch house but in our home in Longmont. In the boys' room, a bullet shot through a whole row of pleats in their drapes, neat as a whistle. When we get to the next life, and I know we will, the angels who greet us will celebrate with relief. They have worked so hard that our gratitude is unbounded.

The pastures were pockmarked with gopher holes, which swallowed so much irrigation water it was difficult to maintain good grass. Just as bad, we lived in fear a horse would step in one, break a leg and throw the rider. The danger inspired Dom to pay the kids a dime for every gopher tail they brought in, and they brought in plenty. Gunfire echoed from the hills and fortunes began to pile up in piggy banks. Paul made $300 one summer. He shot three thousand gophers! Pete, Dave and Joseph kept their earnings secret but they surely had plenty hidden away. Gradually, the rodent population was cut way down, holes were covered over, and things looked better.

There were badger holes, too. Badgers are fearsomely fierce and hungry. To our horror, they grabbed little lambs and hauled them down their burrows. The boys shot them with gleeful vengeance.

Coyotes were another problem, killing far too many sheep, and for a while Dom poisoned them with bait laid in carcasses. He soon found that birds ate it and dropped dead, and a sheep dog got some and died miserably. Game and Fish officials told him that the poison never degrades and spreads ominously. Back to the rifles. A plane was hired, and the Game and Fish people joined Dom to hunt from the air. They shot impressive numbers of the darned critters as they swooped up and down the canyons in the little plane. The ranch became more and more hospitable and productive. The altitude was high enough, at almost eight thousand feet, that rattlesnakes shunned us. McCarty was a blessedly safe haven from dangers, except those we created ourselves.

A den of about thirty rattlers was scared up by the sheep as they were trailed through lower country on the way from McCarty to the desert ranches where they were to spend the fall. The snakes slid out of their den in the rocks in seething masses, their rattling cutting the air hideously. Thank God, not one sheep was a victim, but sheep, horses, dogs and men were terrified.

Overall, however, all seemed to be going well—until an insidious evil cast a shadow. One of the men was sexually aggressive to the girls, really nasty. I begged Dom to get rid of him, but Dom liked him, he was a good worker, and on he stayed until I managed enough fury to finally get him sent far away. My fear for our safety didn't go away, though. Sadly apparent was the fact that the herders, like the sheep, came first in Dom's world.

Dom made it clear that he did not have time to be "nurse maiding" us. I asked for help one day with some little thing, and he said, in an icy voice, "Do not ever ask me to help you. I will not." His attitude towards us, and his behavior, seemed to be insidiously changing. Not only did he neglect us, he began to do some terrible things, better left untold. I was so afraid that his behaviors would slide out of control, I considered taking our children and leaving him, but there was no way I could. Without the sheep it would be impossible to support my children, especially with the expense of cystic fibrosis. I could not manage without Dom, and indeed he could not without me. He told me so, saying, "I could never accomplish what I have without you." We were bound together, and despite my fear, the good of it transcended the difficulties. Our ranches. Our nice homes. Good schools. And Heavens above, no one we knew had as much adventure as we did, and we relished it. For all that, sometimes I wondered how in the world I had ended up with that wild man.

I wasn't the only one. Good friend Dr. Chris Amoroso asked one day, "Soph, what is a nice lady like you doing with those Barbarians?" (Chris was not aware that I was not as nice as I looked.) What indeed? Then I thought of the eight wonderful souls whom Dom and I had given entrance to planet Earth. Whatever else went on, that was the essence of what we were about.

That essence was our part in a Divine Dance. The very dark times had always been wondrously balanced by times of radiant light. Even when chaos confused and abused us, there was no doubt we were part of something grander than we could imagine, and that we were grandly guided.

Married to a man powerfully seductive and, in most ways, wonderful, but with a dark side that was terrifying, I embraced a Don Quixote way of coping. It seemed that the best way to survive would be in the "madness of denial and delusion." Someone wrote, "...in the illusion of reality"—ahh yes! How well that fits. I guess I saw Dom much as Don Quixote saw his lovely Dulcinea. I mostly blocked out what could not be faced.

Required reading at the private high school I attended was Soren Kierkegaard. How lovely to discover Kierkegaard's concept of the hero, or knight, here described:

"The knight of faith, the man who lived in faith, who has given over the meaning of life to his Creator, and who lives centered on the energies of his Maker. He is one who faces his death without a qualm, who is generous, courageous, who touches the lives of others, enriching them, doing nothing to diminish them. He is an ideal, a role model that lifts mankind towards the heroism necessary for his transcendence over his violent world. He also presupposed the fullness of life, the wholeness of being that makes possible the arrival at the time of death a step in the eternal progression rather than a time of terror. Out of terror is born the way to freedom from it. Man is invited to become a knight of faith, a hero, to embrace his part-divinity and in so doing, to be unafraid."

Kierkegaard seemed real, not an illusion at all, and I loved how he soared, and how he provided juxtaposition to Don Quixote's escape from reality. With his lofty concept swirling in my head, I was inspired to get on my horse, grab my lance (figuratively) and joust with the windmills that whirled so menacingly throughout our lives.

One windmill I could not joust: the altitude was not good for Pete. Cystic fibrosis compromises lungs and Pete had trouble keeping his oxygen levels up. He really struggled. Joseph, much younger, also afflicted, had not suffered as much damage, and was able to keep up with everyone and work hard in those first years on the ranch. Francisco, our surrogate grandfather, had taught him to irrigate well enough that he eventually headed the whole operation. On McCarty the air was fresh and fragrant, free of all the things cystics are so vulnerable to, like smog, smoke, dust and microbes. The sun was warm, the food was excellent, and there was peace and lots of love and laughter. For those three or four months of summer, cystic fibrosis, "The Black Cloud," receded somewhat. But as wonderful the ranch was, the altitude became more and more problematic as Pete's, and in just a few years, Joseph's, lungs were progressively compromised by their disease.

When Pete was short of oxygen, it caused real trouble. Anoxia (the deprivation of oxygen) seemed to precipitate something like psychotic breaks. Underlying that, a profound problem, never expressed openly, was fear. Not being able to catch his breath was terrifying. He had spent enough time in hospitals, had seen other children with cystic fibrosis, and had read everything he could lay his hands on, so he knew his hold on life was tenuous. If it came up, I talked about it honestly, as if I tried to cover it up, or make light of it, he would not be able to trust me. Dom would not talk about it at all. Humor, often black, my hope that he could live long and prosper before he died (which Pete slammed me for as "old Ma's bullshit"), and most of all, faith, kept us going.

Fear often comes out as anger. Pete seethed with fury. He was often mad at me and even hated me. Was it that he resented the person who doled out medicine, who did respiratory therapy, pounding on his back and ribs to loosen the gunk in his lungs, and who carted him off to various hospitals? Was he disgusted with me because mothers are supposed to fix everything, and I could not?

My heartbreak would have been utterly devastating if it were not for the other children. They were wonderful. Laughter, often quite inappropriate, was irresistible. (Jokes were so bad a lady as nice as I thought I ought to be shouldn't repeat them, but I relished them.) And I knew they loved me. Somehow I was blessed with the ability to love unconditionally, and Pete's violence and hate never lessened my love for him. Grudgingly, he returned it now and then, times of great joy.

96

Thanks to what Pete taught me, to this day I can love family and friends, no matter how much we may disagree about whatever, or how badly some of us behave, and some of us have behaved outrageously. For me, to overlook differences is not the same as accepting the unacceptable. I cannot cave in to what is wrong, but to rise above it, if there is nothing I can do about it, provides opportunity for a lot more fun and a lot more love. It is a grace to make the most of.

Dom and the boys were working with sheep in the corrals by the barn. Pete, about fifteen and bigger than Dave, was so swept away in his fury that he tried to kill Dave. He had him down in the dust, choking him, when Dom noticed. Dave had turned blue and was almost unconscious. Dom tore Pete off and kicked him across the corral and into the fence. The mental picture of thin, frail Pete, so ill, being slammed across the corral by his dad's boot was shattering, but not as horrible as the vision of beloved little Dave about to die in the dirt. Dom revived Dave. Pete limped to the house. Perhaps it is not surprising that none of us talked about it. Some things are just too dark.

DOM CREATES THE REMUDA

One of Dom's dreams was to have a horse for each of the children so they could ride with him moving sheep and cattle. Dom's friend, Otto Lembcke, bred a fine Arabian stallion with his Morgan and Thoroughbred mares, producing horses with the beauty and intelligence of the Arab and the solid endurance and sensible temperament of the mixed mares. There were two brothers; beautiful little bays with white socks and blazed faces that he thought he could part with to his friend Dom. They took me out to the pasture, honoring my experience with horses, to my surprise and delight, and asked for my opinion. The two little horses trotted up to Otto's call. One look and I fell in love. We bought them for Elaine and Pete, our two oldest children.

Elaine named hers, a year older and a little bigger than Pete's, Barak, which is Hebrew for lightning. Barak sooner or later bucked everyone off, even Elaine. Dom put him with a Basque herder who claimed to be an expert horseman, hoping he could break him of it, but all he did was give the poor horse saddle sores and make him hate herders. Barak got even. He bucked that man off so often he brought him back to Dom turning the air blue with Spanish swear words. Dom was shocked! Spaniards and Basques have created devilishly vile ways of swearing.

Elaine's patience, love and skill rescued Barak. The two were as close as a horse and girl could be. To see Elaine, dark hair flying in the wind, Barak's black mane and tale flying in symphony as they galloped across the ranch was beautiful. She trained him well and he became a wonderful horse.

Pete named his horse Big Enough after his uncle John's childhood horse on Remuda Ranch. Like Barak and Elaine, they were inseparable. Big Enough was quick, sweet and gentle. Pete loved him and rode him well.

Horse-wise I was left behind. I had to check some cattle up on a ridge one day and Pete loaned me Big Enough. I was riding along happily when the little horse made one of his very quick turns and I didn't. There I sat in a clump of sage, with Big Enough looking back at me as if to say, "Well, what the heck happened to you?" He waited for me to climb back on and I hoped I could get away with never telling on myself.

Dom bought horses for the sheep herders and the children at livestock sales in Colorado. Auction horses were a gamble, as a buyer had to go on looks alone. The horses he brought home were good looking and healthy, but getting to know them proved an adventure. Good looking be darned, they provided scares and excitement as behaviors

Dom had no way of seeing at the auction began to emerge. Little eight-year-old Sophie was assigned Red, a big sorrel with white socks and a white blazed face. He jumped the corral fence from a dead stand still. Never had we seen a horse do that! My heart jumped with him in terror, but Sophie hung on and learned to boss him around like a real cowgirl. Her untamed heart went just fine with Red, fairly untamed himself.

Anne's horse was Comanche, a cutting horse that loved to work cattle, one of the best of the whole remuda. Since Anne was next in line for a horse, Dom allowed her to choose. Her heart had already been stolen by the big sorrel and her fervent petition to Heaven was answered. The moment her dad led him up and presented him to her was one of the proudest of her young life. There are moments, words said, events that occur in children's lives that smash them down or lift them up. Sometimes they leave imprints that color their entire lives. Comanche was one of those, a beautiful one, for Anne. She was a middle child, not given the adoration Elaine, the first-born, got from her father and not accorded the attention the littler kids needed. That happens to middle children. Unfair, but I could not help it. Beautiful Comanche provided pride, speed, power and freedom as she galloped across the ranch on him. He was the confidant whose mane received many a whispered secret. He was also the only horse as fast as Paul's Kachina and races were run up and down the ranch at breakneck speed.

David's horse was Bidebe, a big, dark brown who shied at every little thing, leaping this way and that. By the grace of our ever present, hard working guardian angels, Dave stayed on and credits his horse with his excellent horsemanship now. He HAD to learn to ride! And Bidebe was no match for him. Tough and smart, Dave was on top of his big horse in more ways than just physically.

Eagle Feather, lucky horse, was Joseph's. Of all the "remuda," (Spanish name for a string of saddle horses,) he was the biggest and gentlest; Joseph was the littlest. He looked like a peanut up there, but the two of them kept up and worked hard.

Our friends the Schwabachers owned the Quarter Circle 5 ranches in the Pinedale, Wyoming area. In addition to cattle, they raised purebred quarter horses for performance in horse shows and rodeos. A beautiful paint filly got herself tangled up in barbed wire and was badly cut. Dom closed a gaping wound on her side with twenty-two stitches and sewed up another long, deep cut on her front leg. The little horse stood stoically, and Dom so admired her courage that he knew we must have her. It was feared she would be permanently lame, but Dom wanted to take a chance on her.

He had two old horses that needed to be retired. After intense negotiation, he traded them, along with $500 to the Quarter Circle 5 Ranch for the young mare. Such a deal! Dom brought her home and presented her to Paul. It was love at first sight. He named her Kachina.

She was doing well under Paul's training but there was a difficulty with mares. When they went into estrous they became mad for romance. So Kachina, in lusty need, somehow escaped the pasture and took off for the wilds near Brown's Hill, miles south of McCarty, where a mustang stallion welcomed her quite warmly. Dom loaded Dave, Paul, and two horses into the big truck and drove them down to Brown's Hill, unloaded them and left, saying, "Find that damned mare and drive her home! Don't come back without her!" The search was long and hard, they ran out of food and water and were getting desperate. Finally, they found Kachina and drove her romantic little self home along with the whole band of mustangs led by the stallion that had bred her.

The boys wanted to keep the whole herd, but Doc Fulton wisely said most of them probably belonged to neighboring ranchers and we should turn them out. First, Paul tried to ride a Shetland pony stallion that was running with them. He was so mean he bucked Paul off and then went after him, teeth bared and hoofs on the attack. Paul's neck was broken! His head was skewed off to one side, and he was in great pain. By the grace of God, our friends, the Schmids, were visiting. Mike was an osteopathic doctor and he managed to get Paul's skewed neck cracked back in place but he was crippled up for weeks, and has trouble with it still.

As if that were not enough, that darned little stallion managed to perform fascinatingly with a mare in heat. Right there in our front yard he jumped on her to the shock and awe of all. Cousin Poli picked up a steel fence post and whacked that mean little cuss on the head and he dropped dead. You think rodeos are wild? No comparison. Dom opened the gate and sent the boys to drive the herd, except Kachina, back to the wilds.

In time, Kachina gave birth to a beautiful little paint foal. Paul named him Cheechoo. She later presented Paul with a paint filly he named Moriah and with three horses to train, he turned Cheechoo over to Dave. Under Dave's skill he became so gentle he learned how to open the front door and often stomped into our living room to visit and beg for goodies. He liked cookies and he loved us. When Paul or Dave called to him he would come cantering across the pasture, ears pricked up, nickering, happy to see them. The mustang stallion, however, imparted some of his wild DNA and that doggoned Cheechoo took to bolting.

Our horses were loaded into the truck to drive across Wyoming to Cheyenne, where we were to buy sheep from Warren Livestock Company's Pole Creek Ranch. The ranch was miles across and there was riding to be done to round up the bands. We unloaded in the ranch corral and mounted up. Anne, daring and full of mischief got on Cheechoo. For reasons all his own, he broke into a mad gallop headed for disaster, poor Anne yelling frantically, "HELP!" Around the barn he careened, once, twice, three times! Anne's yells advanced to "Whoa, you son-of-a-bitch!" but she held on. It was terrifying but also hilarious and the Echeverria black humor took over, bending us double with laughter. At last he pulled up, sliding in the dust to a stop and Anne was safe though shaken. After that no one would ride him except Paul and Dave. Dave devised a bicycle chain hackamore that sounded cruel, but it worked and Cheechoo was more or less under control.

As usual, I was left behind. Pete was the only one who would let me borrow Big Enough now and then. I longed to join in working cattle and sheep and to ride with my children over our beautiful ranches. Growing up in Arizona, I had fine show horses until I left for college. Wistfully I dreamed Dom would bring me one now.

The fourth of July 1967 was my birthday, and that very afternoon Dom returned from another of his trips to Colorado in his big stock truck. He burst into the house and said, "Come quick and see what I brought you for your birthday!" "My horse, my horse!" I thought, and I dashed behind him to the truck. He opened the big tailgate. I stood, breathless, expecting my horse, but instead down the loading ramp flapped twenty-eight chickens. Chickens! They were very nice chickens, my birthday chickens. "Never look a gift chicken in the beak," I thought, and Dom was so proud of them there was nothing to do but to gush gratitude. We shooed them off to their hen house.

Chickens may be short on brains, but not on personality. Every one of those birds was a character and they added not only to the ambiance of the place but they supplied us with "cackle berries" faithfully every day. And they ate bugs. We grew to love them and we even named them; Mabel, Ethel, Hortense, and so on. I only missed my mythical horse a little.

Sox

Doc Fulton thought it would be better if I were not stuck at home, afoot and unable to help or to check on the kids when they were out working stock on horseback. He arrived one day with his beloved old horse Sox in the back of his pickup truck. "Soph, Sox needs to be on a ranch instead of at my place in town and he would love someone who can ride him. You two can take real good care of each other." I was honored and grateful. Sox was a handsome sorrel with white socks, hence his name, and a pretty white star on his forehead. Joyfully, I threw a saddle on and joined the crew.

There was much to be done. Cattle and sheep had to be moved frequently to prevent over-grazing. They liked to laze around on the meadows near the streams, stomping them to a pulp, and we had to drive them up onto the ridges almost every day. The children had become good cowhands, but I was not that good. There was something about gentle Sox and me that did not intimidate cattle. While we galloped gamely, our speed lacked the aggressiveness the kids had, and my yells and whistles hardly echoed off the hills like theirs did. I cried furious tears of frustration one day as Sox and I drove four hundred Black Angus cows back and forth in front of an open gate they were supposed to go through. They were beautiful cattle, Dom's pride and joy, but Heavens-to-Betsy, they were stupid. One thing after another came up with those darned cows. I couldn't begin to keep up, but Dom and the boys had no trouble at all and those dumb cows grew fat, sleek and profitable.

Some twenty head got nasty foxtail spines in their eyes and were blinded. It must have been terribly painful and they were obviously in distress. Dom grabbed Comanche, Anne's horse, and chased each blinded steer or heifer into a fence, ramming the poor critter so hard in the side with big Comanche that it fell to the ground. Several times Comanche fell too, to his knees, but Dom leaped clear. The kids jumped off their horses and helped hold the critters down, all 800 pounds of them, so Dom could deftly extract the sharp foxtails, apply a quick shot of antibiotic ointment and let them up to trot off bewildered but relieved. They all healed well, thank God yet again.

Sox and I were demoted to sheep herding which was fine with us. Sheep are a lot smarter than cattle and they don't butt or kick. People say they are stupid but that is because they stupidly expect them to be something other than sheep. Those woolly little critters know everything they need to know if they are just allowed to be themselves. We would be wise to extrapolate that to all of us, wouldn't we?

Pilareen

A cousin, Juan Miguel Oroz, was hunting for some stray sheep when he found a tiny fawn nestled under some sagebrush. He did not know that does leave their new babies hidden while they go to water. Thinking she was abandoned, he gently picked her up and brought her to the children. A most adorable little being, she looked up at us with huge, brown eyes, her little black nose twitching, her pink tongue licking us, so trusting and so loving, it was immediate adoration. We fed her from a nipple and bottle we used to feed orphan lambs, holding her in our arms while she eagerly nursed. She could not have been more than a few days old, so small, so delicate, her soft, tan coat

106

sprinkled with white baby spots. I ached for her mother, thinking of her searching for her lost fawn, but there was nothing to be done. Does will not accept fawns that have been handled by people, so to take her back would be her death. If she missed her mother she didn't show it. We were her family from day one. She slept in bed with the children, played with our cats and dogs and wandered up and down the table when we ate, sticking her little nose up to cadge treats. Her favorites were bacon and banana peels, quite odd, but we never argued with her. Very soon she began going on our hikes with us, bounding along with our dogs and our hiking cats.

Unusual as it was, our cats, Ridiculous, Felix, Cosmo and Motor Ball liked to hike with us. They followed along, often checking out what might be interesting, and then, not wanting to lose us, their heads would pop up out of the tall sage like Jack-in-the-boxes to see where we were.

In the evenings when we sat out on the bench in front of the house Pilareen danced for us, leaping and prancing up and down the yard, utterly enchanting. As she grew she became independent and disappeared sometimes for days. What sorrow! What worry! Then here she came, hungry for her bottle, bounding joyfully up to us and telling of her adventures with her big eyes, her twitching tail and her lovely, soft ears. Her body language was easy to read.

When fall came and it was time to go back to Longmont for school, Dom found a friend who had an antelope fawn. He would take Pilareen for the winter and care for her with the little antelope since we

107

could not have her in Longmont by city ordinance. Our hearts broke as we drove off. Pilareen raced after the station wagon until we outran her. Dom jumped in his truck and followed to catch her. It was so awful, some of us cried for days.

She disappeared before Dom could take her to his rancher friend. Chato, the Basque in charge of the ranch in our absence, loved her. He tied a large red bandanna around her neck to protect her from hunters, as it was that dreadful season. (Hunters, except a few friends, were hated. They left beer cans, whiskey bottles and trash behind, stole stuff, cut fences and spooked the sheep.) One day Pilareen was gone. Chato said he searched the whole ranch for her but he could find no trace. It was against the law to keep wildlife as pets, and the game warden knew we had her. A friend, he had managed not to notice. I embraced a dream that he had taken her to the National Park where she would live happily ever after. I needed to believe that and did until Dom announced at dinner a few weeks later that she had been shot. Her little body was found behind the barn. Everyone melted away from the table to grieve in heartbroken privacy----the only time Dom's strict rule that no one leaves the table was allowed to be broken. To this day we can still cry about it.

The Lives of Herders and Lives of Sheep

Sox and I didn't have a lot of sheep herding to do. We mostly just visited the herders to check on them and pick up their shopping lists. A herder, usually a Basque, would invite me to join him for a cup of marvelous coffee, brewed in his blue enamel camp pot on his little stove, laced with honey and canned milk. I began to pick up Spanish as they picked up English.

There were also a few Mexicans, best of all Francisco, who headed up the irrigating and was a veritable grandfather to the kids. Obviously he had been a man of stature in Mexico. He had an aura of dignity and integrity, enhanced by the sparkle in his eyes and his mane of snow-white hair. He especially loved young Joseph and taught him how to irrigate the hay meadows and many other wise things only a grandfather could teach. He turned up every morning with fresh milk from our cow and he made delicious tortillas for us.

The lives of herders were all about being out in the wilds with only their horses, their dogs, and the sheep for company. Their homes were the famous Wyoming sheep wagons; wonderfully designed, compact, oblong boxes with rounded roofs of canvas or tin mounted solidly on big wheels. They were configured so trucks or teams of horses could pull them into rough country where they provided shelter and comfort in all kinds of weather. A platform in the back with a little window over it made a cozy bed. A small wood stove, good enough to bake great mounds of delicious sheepherder bread, ubiquitous beans, mutton with plenty of garlic, and rice pudding, stood near the front door, a bin for firewood beside it. Drawers and cabinets were ingeniously placed. A pullout table between two benches that sat on top of storage bins made a little dining room. We cooked many meals and spent nights in the little camps when there was work to be done, and the crews were gathered away from the ranch.

Some crafty sheep ranchers from eastern Wyoming took it into their heads to market them. They sheathed one in copper roofing, outfitted the insides with luxurious Ralph Lauren linens, china, and some lovely art, put it up on the balcony of an art studio on the square in Jackson Hole, and sold it for $40,000. Hallelujah! Sheep wagons are desirable items now, but not ours. We have managed to refurbish two of our old ones and park them where numerous little Echeverrias can camp in them, but somehow we have not managed any $40,000 deals.

Bands were gathered for sorting lambs when it was time to wean them from their mothers. Elaine, Anne, and little Sophie were charged with holding lambs as the men docked their tails and castrated the males. There they were, with blood spattered over their beautiful faces and down their shirt fronts. Then with speed and efficiency the girls stamped paint brands on each sheep. Dom and I were proud of their skills but would such accomplishment be socially acceptable elsewhere? What is socially acceptable anyway? We were too busy doing what we loved to care.

Basques, a few Greeks, an occasional Peruvian and Mexicans seemed to be the only people who could endure what herding sheep entailed. It is in Basque DNA to be tough and proudly independent. That powerful independence has also been getting them in trouble with the Spanish government from the time Spain and France, by treaty, ran their shared border down the middle of the seven Basque Provinces. That action denied the Basques their treasured autonomy and ETA was formed, a fierce, mysterious, revolutionary group. ETA stands for "Euskadi Ta Askatasuna" which is Basque for "Land and Liberty." One of our herders, Cookie, which they spelled "Kuque," was hiding out in wild Wyoming with us, a man with a price on his head just like Andres Irustia, both fugitive members of the ETA.

Kuque was not the only brush we had with ETA. Years later, I was in London and bought a newspaper. Right there, on the front page, was a story about captured ETA terrorists who were to be tried and sentenced. The picture showed four young women who looked alarmingly like our very own daughters, except they had short hair. Their name was Echeverria, and one was even Elaine Echeverria. Was the family in big trouble? We checked with our cousins in Spain and they denied knowing anything about it. But did they?

For our foreign workforce, sheepherding was a career to be proud of. It wasn't a career (or even a job) for your usual every day unemployed white guy. No way. They seemed to prefer almost anything else, no matter how lowly. Perhaps they cringed at the prejudice long held against sheep men who arrived in the west speaking only Spanish. They looked different and they were different, and as often happens in established societies, difference is looked down upon. Myths were created to further slander them.

Cattlemen thought that sheep would take up their range and would grub grass down to the roots. Cattle and any animal, even wild game will grub to the ground if they run out of forage. They will struggle to get what they need. The fault is with the operators who

111

allow overgrazing, sometimes unable to avoid it in times of draught, but never with hungry livestock. That fact was ignored, and sheep continued to be blamed. There were areas in Wyoming that cattle had so overgrazed that the grass had given up, the land to be taken over by cactus, and not one sheep had ever been there. That fact seems to have been overlooked.

Another myth chewed on by cattlemen, and those who hung on their every word, was that sheep and cattle were incompatible. The truth was that they complemented each other. Sheep ate young shoots of plants poisonous to cattle, like Larkspur, if they were put on the range in early spring. They also grazed off the dreadful foxtail spines before they matured. Cattle ate the tougher, higher grasses that sheep spurned. The combination was excellent, and we ran our cattle and sheep together successfully.

The Law of the West (or Not)

In the Spring of 1969, Jose Mari, Dom's foreman and right-hand man, drove into McCarty to ask Dom about some cattle he spotted on the southeast end of Echo Springs Ranch. He said, "I didn't know you bought cattle. They look pretty good, down there near that tank with the only tree on the ranch." "WHAT?" exclaimed Dom. "We better go check that out! I haven't bought a single cow since we sold ours a year ago!"

The cattle did indeed look good; happily grazing on our fine grass near the pond with the lonesome, brave cottonwood. Their brand belonged to old George Salisbury, a big cattleman from Savery, down near Baggs, Wyoming. His ranch shared a fence line with ours, and Dom and Jose Mari found where it had been neatly snipped to let the cattle through. When they got home and told us about it, we quickly got up in arms, ready to start a range war with George. Dom said, "Let's be neighborly and not cause any bad blood. Friends are more useful than enemies. Come fall, we will just avail ourselves of some really good beef to feed us through the winter." And so we did. George must have accepted it as a solution better than war with Dom Echeverria, if the old bird even had a good enough count to know a couple of steers were missing.

Top: A large bull is unloaded on McCarty Canyon Ranch. We utilized premium stock to improve the quality of our cattle herd. Bottom: Dom in his Borcelino Hat at the auction in Casper, WY. He bought the ranches at the auction.

.

Elaine branding sheep with the Lazy YS brand. However hard ranch life was at times, the author believes it helped her children become confident and self-sufficient.

Opposite page, top: Sheep graze the meadows at McCarty Canyon Ranch. The ranch barn is in the background, and our little home sits under the "Mother Cottonwood," the only tree at the homestead. Bottom: McCarty Canyon Ranch in the fall.

This page, top: Two Basques work sheep near the barn. Bottom: The Grand "Mother Cottonwood," home to chattering birds by days and twinkling stars by night.

Top: An historic shot of the backyard at McCarty Canyon Ranch: it is the only time it was mowed. Opposite page, top: Bridge across the creek in the backyard of the main ranch house, a lovely spot that routinely attracted kids and ducks. Bottom: Pete and Paul herd ducks to the ranch house for the night so the coyotes wouldn't get them. The boats are made of feed troughs.

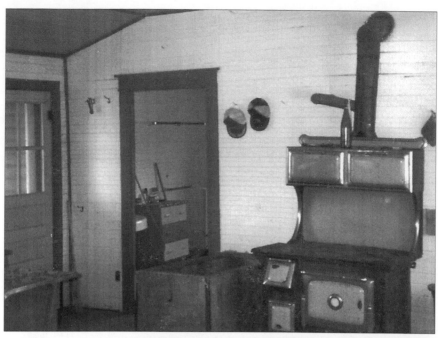

Opposite page, top: Woodstove in the main ranch house. It took some "understanding," but it worked great. Bottom: Our long kitchen table—or half of it!—was the scene of many great feasts. It was always decorated with wildflowers, beer and wine. This page: The boys' room was heated by a woodstove. The bookcase to the left was where the hawk took up residence.

Opposite page, top: The author in the ranch living room, with it's great Buck stove. Bottom: Pigs Junio and Pablo, great pets until they grew up and started acting like pigs. They frequently broke into the kitchen and chased its occupants around until they were fed. The author solved the problem by eating them.

This page, top: Bath time at McCarty involved a dip in the creek. Bottom: A cousin and Elaine enjoy a refreshing skinny dip on a hot summer day.

123

This page, top: Joseph herding goats up the lane with Cheechoo following, hoping for handouts in the living room. Bottom: McCarty Canyon Barn seen from a nearby ridge, with sheep in the meadow.

Opposite page, top: Ewes and lambs grazing happily on McCarty Canyon Ranch. Bottom: The kids herding sheep on the ranch.

This page, top: The little coal house, used as a bedroom for bum (orphan) lambs. Goats, pictured here, provided their milk. Opposite page, top: The author climbed Rendle Butte and snapped this photo of Dude Canyon and the ridge beyond. Bottom: The view from Buffalo Ridge, looking up Dude Canyon.

127

Top: Castle Rocks, a formation on McCarty Canyon Ranch where we discovered an eagle's nest, shown in the bottom picture.

Top: Time for a break in a hot hike! Anna and assorted beloved dogs enjoy dipping into a cool pool. Bottom: Two little hikers walk a wooded trail through the ranch.

129

This page, top: Joseph; Ven Barclay's African Ridgeback, Wrinkles; Sophie and Dulaney Barclay atop Dulaney Butte, Wyoming. Bottom: The author, a Wyoming Woman.

Opposite page, top: The McCarty Canyon Ranch house at a distance, seen from Buffalo Ridge. Bottom: Paul's Hill on McCarty. Everyone had a special place on the ranch. When Paul was little, he requested, "Sprinkle my ashes there!"

This page, top: Dom, with little Joseph in front, and Paul ride the ranch. Opposite page, top: Pete's Big Enough, one of two half Arabian horses we bought from Otto Lembcke. Bottom: Cowboy Joseph in a big hat and big saddle, ready to work!

134

Opposite page, top: School buddy Jay Neighbors, Pete, Paul and Anne ready to ride. Bottom: Darling friend Mary Beth Schmid, on Joseph's horse Eagle Feather.

This page, top: Anne on wonderful Comanche. Bottom: Elaine's horse, Barak, purchased from Otto Lembcke's ranch near Laramie, WY.

This page, top: Paul, Anne and Joseph with Kachina, herder Basilio Arregui and Fagmo the ram. Fagmo bonded with horses and would have nothing to do with sheep. (He was a failure as a breeder, thus the name Fagmo). Bottom: Paul getting bucked off a cranky Shetland pony

Opposite page, top: Kachina with her colt, Cheechoo. Bottom: Cheechoo grew up as part of the family and often came in the house for meals. Dave obliged.

Opposite page, top: Paul with Kachina at a sheep camp. Bottom: Cheechoo stands next to a propane tank we bought for cooking and to power the ranch refrigerator. The tank was big and ugly, but such a help. This page, top: Dear friend Cindy Schmid and Anne, on Anne's Big Red.

Top: Joseph in bed with Rediculous the cat, Pilareen and Mayi, the little family dog. Bottom: Pilareen does in the flower arrangement in the living room.

Top: Dewy and Mavis Brown's little ladies feed Pilareen. Bottom: Sophie Dominik (Little Soph) relaxes with Cosmo Cat, Pilareen and a guinea piglette.

Wyoming to Colorado:
Moving with the Seasons

In late August, the land began to whisper that all too soon it would be time to leave. The Aspen leaves, still green, somehow sounded different as they quaked in the breeze. Flowers went to seed, preparing for next spring when they would burst forth again. Now and then we could hear a bull elk bugling his otherworldly call, summoning his ladies for fall mating. The antelope on Siberia Ridge and Sourdough ranches began to gather in their magnificent herds for fall breeding and migration. The horses first grew beards, and then their sleek coats began to thicken into winter "furs." Birds flocked together, planning their trips south. A new time, a new beginning, was upon us, always exciting but at the same time sad. While Longmont was good to us, it was never the home of our hearts the way Wyoming was.

We packed in preparation for our exodus. Hunting season made it easier. When hunters began to impose their noisy, messy, drunken selves on the land it was so offensive we needed to escape. When we left after our first summer, those damned hunters stole almost everything of interest or value from our home. The ranch had come with some great stuff, like butter churns, branding irons, ancient cookware and old pictures. We had taken our Navajo rugs and our valuable things, but the ancient treasures were simply gone when we got back the next spring. As time to leave approached again, I painted a sign that said, "Welcome to our home. Please be kind to it. If you want to take any of our stuff, please know that you can get stuff just like it, really cheap, at garage sales, like we did. Have fun! Good hunting!"

It worked fairly well, and one bunch even left a thank-you note and a bottle of Scotch. Alas, the sign must have been irresistible, as after a year or two it was gone, and things went to hell again.

The time came to order trucks, gather the sheep and move everything to farms around Longmont for the winter. Big triple decked semis drove up, and we began loading the sheep, top decks first, then the middle, and last, the bottom. The kids, as always, were the best help. If sheep were too crowded, they would smother each other, and if they were too loosely loaded, they wouldn't support each other when the trucks moved. Our foremen hitched the Wyoming wagons to their pickups, I loaded the station wagon, called the dogs, cats, and kids and away we all went.

The Colorado farmers were glad to see us again. The sheep cleaned up the remains of harvested crops, sprinkled their excellent fertilizer generously, and aerated the ground with their sharp little hooves. The herding was more demanding, as the bands had to be contained closely, especially when we had to drive them from where they were unloaded to their pastures. Sometimes it did not go well.

Dom was trailing a band of about 1200 sheep down a county road when a farmer dashed out in front of them, waving his arms, yelling, "Get those sheep back! They will get off the road into my pasture!" Of course, with his waving and yelling, the sheep left the road and went into his pasture. Dom, in a fury, ran towards him and scared him so badly he fell to the ground and began to crawl away, whereupon Dom booted him in the rear. Unfortunately, the farmer was recovering from hemorrhoid surgery and his agony was acute. Someone called the sheriff who arrested Dom on the spot and hauled him off to jail in Greeley. The sheep went wild. Dom's one permitted phone call was to the bank that carried our line of credit, and bless their hearts, they dashed to the scene and bailed Dom out. Dom called me to get the kids out of school to come round up the sheep and rescue him. No surprise, the farmer tried to sue, but there was no chance he would win since he had precipitated the whole mess. We recaptured the sheep, drove them to their pasture, and got Dom home, still fuming. Civility, kindness, the attributes I so valued, seemed far away, and yet the sheep were where they should be, we had survived yet again, and I reminded myself, as I often do, "All is well, all is very well."

When we were short of herders Dom would leave Paul, Pete, Dave, and sometimes Elaine with the sheep until late at night. They kept warm by building fires of whatever they could find. They dug up potatoes the farmers had missed harvesting, roasted them in their little fires, and that was all they had to eat. Dom said he had not abandoned them; he was just too busy to get back. I had no idea where they were, and could not have found them, so I worried, waited, and prayed. The kids seemed to think it was just fine. They understood how demanding the sheep business was and they admired how hard their Dad worked. There was also a huge pay-off. Those kids knew how to survive.

Dog Stories and Doggone Stories

At 2:45 a.m. on a winter morning, the phone rang. A sheriff said dogs had terrified one of our bands, and the sheep had stampeded onto the interstate freeway. There were sixty-eight dead sheep and many more injured lying all over the road. Two big semi-trucks and five cars were wrecked and traumatized motorists were yelling and shaking their fists, threatening lawsuits. Police cars with flashing lights and blaring sirens were lined up, the police trying to establish order. Dom dashed to the scene to drag dead sheep off the highway and to shoot those badly injured to put them out of their agony. What was left of the band was rounded up and returned to Ray Elmquist's farm. The marauding dogs were shot. Motorists were sent on down the road by the highway patrol. The damage was not sufficient to warrant going to court, and the police just wanted to get things cleaned up. Around dawn Dom returned, shaken.

Sometimes dogs from nearby towns and farms formed packs

145

and harassed the sheep, despite fierce defense by our sheep dogs. Dom gave the herders guns and told them to shoot, but carefully, as if it could not be shown that the dogs were actually attacking, we could end up in jail. There were a few harrowing incidents when attacks were stopped with gunshots. Farmers dashed in, yelling bloody murder, but they always had to back down, and, in several instances, they had to pay us damages. For all that, Dom was well liked and respected, and he continued to find good farms for our bands. Some of those farmers are friends to this day.

As well as our small pet dogs, we had big sheep dogs, probably thirty or forty of them over the years, that helped us work the bands. My favorite was Chispas, a big, furry Border collie mix, who, Dom said, had the intelligence of a seven-year old child. All the other dogs—Napoleon, Hippy, Chowdie, Buddy, Olivia, Prince (who was one), and Francisco—thought I was their mother. They clustered around my legs, refusing to even look at a sheep while I was there. Not Chispas! I would point to a straying ewe and say, "Chinga-le," the Spanish command for "Get it." (Actually I was told recently that it means something really, really bad, so let us abandon that. No wonder the Basques laughed when I said it.) Chispas would dash to the wanderer, circle her, and bring her back to the band with a look that said, "I did it!" He seemed to know everything. Joseph and I came to believe that dogs are connected to the Cosmic Consciousness. Their actual brains are not very large, but dogs, especially dogs like Chispas, know EVERYTHING. When we pay attention, look into their eyes, and read their body language, it is plain to see their knowledge and their wisdom, which is vast.

As much as we loved our dogs, Dom did not. He was leaving to drive sheep and needed a dog. He picked Chispas up, roughly, and as he threw him into the back of the truck, Chispas yelped in pain and nipped at him. Dom snarled at Dave, "Go get my pistol." Fear swept over Dave, but he handed his Dad the gun. Dom shot our most beloved Chispas dead right in front of Paul and Dave. He dumped him on the lawn, and snorted, "He is too old to work, and I don't want anything around that doesn't work." The boys asked, "Dad, why couldn't you let him come home with us and be a happy old porch dog? We really loved him!" Dom said nothing and drove off. Dave confessed sadly that sometimes he wondered if his Dad would shoot him. Good God!

Dom was merciless. Everything and everyone had to be useful. His priority was practicality and woe to anyone who didn't toe his mark. Making plenty of money to meet his family's material needs was always first and foremost. Sentimentality, a distraction and impediment, had no place in his way of thinking.

He did not like my little dog Mayi, who was good for nothing but love, and one day when I was not home he stole her away. He told me when I began to search for her that he had taken her out to the sheep. He said, "She didn't like it out there and ran away. She's gone." Paul and Dave said their dad shot her. The image of her little face, her kindly brown eyes, terrified as he dragged her away, just about wrecked me. Then a wicked thought intruded. How good it

147

would have been to see his brown eyes as terrified as my little dog's must have been as I aimed my pistol at him. Oh my God! It was not like me to have such a dark and dreadful fantasy! Or was it?

My fantasy became almost obsessive when Dom took Anne's adorable little dog, Moki, Mayi's son, to our feedlot, just as he had Mayi. Because Moki slept with Anne, under the covers, he was doomed. Anne and I hurried to the feedlot to try to find him, and there he was, lying wounded and bleeding. He had been savaged by the big sheep dogs and was near death. Anne could hardly breathe as she cradled him in her arms until he died. She apologized to her dear little friend for what had happened to him, for his pain and suffering, for her inability to save him from Dom.

Her heart went out to all suffering animals, and when Dom, in a fury, stomped a ewe almost to death, Anne rushed to her and held her head as she gasped her last breath, apologizing again for what Dom had done. The wounds his cruelty inflicted on the animals we loved were devastating to her. When people behave shamefully and do not own it, the shame will be carried by those close to them, and the shame of her father's actions was carried by Anne deep into adulthood. I, on the other hand, felt utter sorrow and murderous fury. Was Dom oblivious, sadistic? What could I have done for Anne? For me? We were trapped in a terrible, dark storm. My "shoot Dom" fantasy recurred with a frightening vengeance.

I engaged a psychiatrist to help me as I was "on the verge of standing more than I could bear," again. He expressed concern about

148

how adamantly I denied and buried anger. Finally, I got up the courage to confess that at times I had fantasies of violent retribution. I wanted so much to be who I hoped was my true self, a kind and gentle person who healed, who nurtured, who forgave, and who brought light and laughter. Yet there I was, fantasizing with evil relish about shooting Dom in the head.

The psychiatrist said, "Thank God you created those fantasies! I was afraid you would implode with all the anger you must have. Your fantasies have been a saving release. No shame, just don't act on them." He impressed upon me that to be real, to be authentic, I had to face my anger and find appropriate ways to express it. A huge weight was lifted. I felt authentic. But how to express anger appropriately? What a challenge! My feisty friend Doreen Mora came to mind.

Doreen was famous for creatively blowing steam. About 4'11' and Philippine, she was a dangerous little bundle of energy. Before she moved next door to us in Longmont, she had been married to Joe, a bar owner in Casper, Wyoming. Tales were told about how when old Joe made her mad she would get in her convertible and cruise around Casper shooting street lights out. I was impressed. I was even more impressed when her beautiful daughter, Katrina, told about the night a rough kind of guy followed her home from the bar. Katrina said, and I quote, "She couldn't get rid of him so she shot him and went to bed. The next morning the cops rang her door bell and said, 'Doreen, there is a wounded guy lying out in the street who says you shot him.' 'What? You mean the son of a bitch didn't die?' she asked, and the

cops said, 'No, he didn't. You need to sharpen up your aim, Doreen.'"
Katrina thought it was funny, unperturbed about the whole event, as
though that is what a woman would naturally do. It sounded appropriate, given the circumstances and the location, but I supposed
it would not do for me, even if I was a Wyoming Woman.

Family Time, Sort of

Dom came in the kitchen door and sat down at the head of the
table for supper. Between bites, he said, as though he was telling us
about the weather, "I just bought the Forty Four Ranch from a doctor in
California. It's contiguous to Echo Springs on the south, with Hanson's
ranch and the railroad tracks bordering it on the north. Should make a
great addition to that range as it gives us seventeen miles, north-south,
and twelve east-west." He was so "hip-slickin' cool," as the kids said
back then, that no one said much more than, "Oh." Or, "Oh?" He re-
named it "Lazy Y S," which was the brand he acquired when he was
seventeen years old and his dad had given him a small bunch of steers.
The addition of the Lazy Y S Ranch gave us a lot more grazing land,
and saved us from much traipsing over Wyoming and Colorado. So, in
the late 60's, Dom was less pressured and stayed home more, catching
up on the reading he loved and spending time with his children.

Dom even found time to go to a niece's wedding in Reno,
Nevada. Beautiful Susan was to marry a handsome banker. It was
sure to be wonderful, as Echeverria celebrations were events not to
be missed. As usual, there was a great last minute scurry of throw-

150

ing things in suitcases and giving orders to the men who were to "hold the fort" and watch the kids.

We sped out of the ranch to catch a plane in Rock Springs. Dom was tired and asked me to drive so he could sleep. About the time we reached the Red Desert Station, miles after we had passed Wamsutter, he woke up and said, "Where are Juan and Poli? You were to pick them up in Wamsutter!" "Holy Molasses, Dom, you did not tell me!" "Well, I forgot. Whip a 'U' and go back and get them!" I whipped the U, looking both ways as I broke the law, and sped back to the little town where our cousins were waiting. They jumped in, and I stepped on the gas, revving up to 110 miles per hour, which was as fast as the station wagon would go. No one said a word. We skidded to a halt on the airport tarmac next to our plane, its propellers already spinning, and the stairs about to be pulled up. "Wait! Wait!" we yelled, and they did. I handed the station wagon keys to someone, wondering if we would ever see it again.

We were the only passengers, and the stewardesses were happy to have us on board. They were "chilling out," recovering from their previous passengers. They latched on to us, twinkling and twitching for dashing Dom, as women so often did. They needed to vent. "Those people were the worst slobs, the rudest, most ill-mannered people we ever had to deal with! They ordered us around, threw their trash on the floor, and complained about everything!" (Actually, they were so famous that I had better not mention their names.) We ordered drinks for all of us to aid their recovery and the flight turned out to be a delightful party.

In Vernal, Utah, we changed planes and were sitting on the runway waiting for take-off. As the plane revved up, a lot of sawdust flew out of the engine right by our window. I started to get up and said, "I'm out of here!" Dom held me down and wouldn't let me leave. He was not someone to do battle with, so I segued to silent prayers, sitting there as he held my arm painfully, while the engine spewed stuff. Thank God, it was announced we had to change planes!

There was no airline to Reno, so Dom chartered a little putt-putt plane, so small we had to take the wedding present, a big sheep skin rug, out of its box so that Poli could hold it on his lap. We were crammed in! Groaning along, the plane barely cleared a ridge of mountains, pine trees almost stroking the bottom. Holy perilous merde! But it got us to Reno, the wedding was gorgeous, the family delightful, and all was well.

The flight home was terrifying, as we ran into a hellacious hail storm, the plane bucking and swerving, hail pounding it noisily, but we landed at the Rock Springs airport just fine. Our station wagon was waiting there, and back to the ranch we went. Staying home seemed wonderful.

WE SPREAD OUR WINGS AND FLY

There was a part of Dom, the bright, light part that wanted to transcend the old, hard ways and to do wonderful things for us. In the summer of 1969 he took the seven children and me to the Basque country. He wanted us to know our Basque family and the land that gave birth to the Echeverrias. Also, secretly, I think he wanted to show us off to them.

At the time we were to fly to Spain, Elaine was a student at Lincoln School in Providence, RI, the same fine, private girls' school her grandmother and I had attended. She belonged to the school glee club, and had been promoted to the exclusive Lambrequins. That summer they gave concerts throughout Europe and competed successfully in an International Competition in Wales, and we were to join them in Paris.

Dom and my mother did not get along well. My uppity family disapproved of him and well he knew it, but he rose above that with generosity and courage and he invited her to come with us. My mom was one wise lady. She expressed gratitude to him and then announced, "WHY would I want to go to Europe when I haven't even seen the rest of Arizona?" We wondered what she was really up to. She had told, with relish, of her friend who said she just wanted to curl up in bed with a good book, but she couldn't find one, but she did find a fellow who said he had read one, which worked just fine.

Mon Dieu! Quelle Aventure!

We flew from Denver to New York, the first leg of our trip to Spain, so excited we could hardly sit still. The first stop was The City, amazing to our Western eyes, where we spent a night. Then it was time to head for JFK! We had chosen Icelandic Airways because they charged only $100 each, New York to Europe, and out across the tarmac in the dead of night we headed for our plane. It was parked so far away it was almost to Iceland already. On we got and off we flew to Reykjavik where we were held captive in the air terminal while a Russian military plane landed. The Cold War was going full blast and security was tight. The boys were thrilled, ready to do something dramatic about it. Good God, what? We girls escaped to the airport stores.

Iceland was a place to be explored. Dramatic topography sheathed in green grass, or was it moss?—with wonderful Icelandic horses and great woolly sheep, it beckoned to us—but the Russians were coming, leaping lizards! The military plane landed with Russian markings, but nothing came of it and after about eight hours of waiting apprehensively off we went to Luxembourg.

Dom rented a little, blue Ford minibus and ordered me to drive because as foreigners, wandering around lost, we might be stopped and I was more likely to beguile the police out of arresting us. (I enjoyed a sort of fame for being able to do that.) With apprehension I asked an airport guard who spoke no English, "Paris?" He pointed southwest, anyway I hoped it was southwest, and I stepped on the gas.

Dom and David shared a fascination with World War II and the Holocaust and wanted to explore Germany. The rest of us overruled them and we managed to miss that tortured country entirely. An ancient hotel in Belgium was our shelter for the first night. We sank into deep feather beds, snoozed away, and were greeted in the morning with Belgium coffee and croissants so heavenly we remember them still!

Reims, a wondrous cathedral built over a period of years in the Middle Ages, was the next stop. Awesome was what it was, and we thought of the degree of faith that must have existed to inspire the wealthy to finance such an immense undertaking, and for everyone who worked on it to do what they did. Brilliant engineering and marvelous architecture, crowned with art that may have rivaled the Louvre had our heads spinning. It seemed that a Higher Power must have participated for something so gorgeous to be created. The Presence definitely could be felt. On to Paris!

In wonder, we drove through Parisian neighborhoods with no idea where we were or of how to get to the hotel to meet the Lambrequins. Dom said, "You look nice and friendly, so get out, go down

155

the sidewalk and find someone who can speak English." I walked while he drove along behind me. "Do you speak English?" I asked again and again and was so coldly rebuked that I began to wonder if I had spinach in my teeth or if I really looked all that nice and friendly. A priest came along, a slight little man in a long, brown cassock and a merry smile. "Do you speak English?" I asked pleadingly. "Non," he said, but somehow we understood each other enough so that Dom showed him the address of the hotel. He nodded smilingly, hopped in the front seat and by golly he got us there. Did he have wings and a little halo that we couldn't quite see? I think he must have.

Elaine's singing group was there, all fluttery and lovely, full of stories about their summer across Europe and the British Isles. We were given a private dining room for a splendid feast and our own recital. They sang gorgeously in several languages, all classical music, and we were ecstatic. Elaine was a soprano with a wonderful voice and there she stood, so lovely her brothers and sisters were uncharacteristically impressed. They often called her "Mother Chicken," because she was cluckingly bossy. In Paris she was a swan.

We sailed down the Seine, singing and euphoric. The Lambrequins flew off to America leaving Elaine with us, and we ventured out to see that celebrated city. The Louvre loomed ahead and Dom parked our little bus in front. He sat there, uncharacteristically fearful, just looking at it. "Don't get out!" he commanded. He was sure the children would get lost, or worse, one of them, probably Pete, would deface the Mona Lisa or some other marvelous work of art. There we sat, parked in front of that famous museum, surely the only people ever to suffer such an inauspicious non-happening.

However, it was obvious we were not slopping up the wonder and the magic of Gay Pareee. We could find no one who could speak English in the rather lowly venues we stayed in. The famous shops eluded us, which was probably a good thing. Dom, still appropriately apprehensive, nixed the Eiffel Tower. Paul said just the other day that he is still mad they did not get to the top of it. Our hotel was about a one-star, if that. But it did have a TV in the lobby, which was playing a John Wayne western dubbed in French. The Duke in French? Culture shock! We decided we needed to get out of town.

Rambouillet, where the breed of our most prized sheep originated, beckoned. The drive out of Paris was terrifying, with roundabouts and everyone round-abouting every which way, lickity split. The commotion scared me so I could not drive, no matter my ability to schmooze police. Dom took over and did terrifyingly wild maneuvering and we escaped. Suddenly, in a country swathed in green fields we saw sheep! It was the high point of France for Dom.

Versailles delighted us and we wandered around with our mouths agape all day. The kids were sufficiently artistic that they could appreciate the paintings, the architecture, and the furniture—art everywhere, beyond anything we had ever seen. I regaled them with the story of our French ancestors, the De Chapotins, who surely had been where we now stood, as they were among the nobility and would have been at court with the royals. Had Sophie and Clementine De

Chapotin sat in those very same gilt chairs, elegantly placed along a richly tapestried wall? Had they danced in the grand ballroom, reflected in the floor-to-ceiling mirrors? Legend has it they were so high up in the French court that during the Revolution they were to be sent to the guillotine with King Louis XVI and Queen Marie Antoinette. They escaped by crawling down a ditch in the dead of night to Nice, where they boarded a ship bound for America. They must have been good at crawling as they left with plenty of money and the family crest.

Most of the French people we encountered did not take to us, even though we dressed well and the children behaved nicely. We caught just enough of what they were saying to gather they found us appalling, insane to have so many children and to take them traveling. We seem to have been pegged as lowly, uncivilized American tourists. At that time, American tourists had earned the unpleasant label of "Ugly Americans." (Is it better now? Are we not so ugly or are the French mellower?) We left for Lourdes.

A Few Little Miracles

Our nuns and priests in Colorado had urged us to visit Lourdes to pray for cures for Pete and Joseph. The miracles that had taken place there were well documented, and I had read a book about Saint Bernadette that told of her wondrous visions of the Blessed Virgin and her miraculous spring that healed many who bathed in it. To this day medical miracles are documented, rarely, but they do happen. There were other amazing miracles in Bernadette's time. The

158

sun stood still and spun in the sky one afternoon with sixty thousand pilgrims watching. Holy Mary appeared again and again to Bernadette. Her messages, faithfully relayed, were what one would expect. Essentially, clean up your act, folks, or disaster will befall you.

The Catholic Church, always slow to respond, put her through holy—well, unholy, hell, until they could no longer deny the validity of who she was, all she had witnessed, and the miracles bestowed. She was canonized and Lourdes was sanctified as a holy place. A grand cathedral was built and baths to accommodate hundreds of pilgrims were installed with the holy spring water piped in. All of this was revealed in the movie, "The Song of Bernadette," with Jennifer Jones exquisitely playing Bernadette. I believed the story. The children and even Dom believed it too, in their own ways.

The prayed-for cure for Pete and Joseph I regarded wistfully as perhaps possible. I have always had a sense that our three sons, afflicted with cystic fibrosis, were here on Earth to accomplish Something. If the belief that we choose our life missions is true, then to ask for a change in theirs seemed suspect, though I could not help hoping they could be cured. After all, life missions can be altered, and in fact, couldn't their alteration be part of their missions?

Dom would not talk about feelings, "mushy crap" or "holy stuff," so he remained mostly aloof. The baths were clearly distasteful to him, yet he had a deep faith, mostly hidden. He was so busy he rarely made it to Mass, and when he did he sat in a back pew, fell asleep and entertained us with loud snoring. The kids would nudge

159

each other and whisper, "He's here! Only Dad can snore like that!"

He demanded that I go to Mass wherever we were, and that I take any children not working with him. He believed my prayers kept us safe and once when a disaster hit the sheep, he blamed me because I had missed Mass and failed to pray enough. With grains of salt was how I took that. At Lourdes he was in foreign territory, unsure of what to think or how to act. One of our unusually perceptive children wondered if he was afraid it might be such a holy place that the darkness he knew lurked inside him would be exposed. Holy shadow sides! Could that be true of all of us?

Nuns in black habits with white wimples swooped down upon us and to our horror stripped most of us, even Dom, to our birthday suits as we yelled, "Non! Non!" Their strength and efficiency were astounding. They shoved us like livestock into long, cement pools just like the troughs Dom dipped sheep in. Anne was terrified and remembers how the water stank and how threateningly murky it was. She put up such a fight the nuns gave up on her and she escaped. Only Pete and Joseph were to have been blessed by the holy spring water but somehow those holy dervishes got us dumped in so fast our heads spun. I thought of all the sick people who had just been run through the very same water and said a fervent prayer for the miracle that we didn't catch anything. It worked. We came out somewhat dirtier but healthy enough.

As we emerged dripping from the baths, Paul and Dave zoomed out of there so fast we didn't even see them. Pete and Joseph

160

followed, escaping the nuns' clutches while Dom and I retrieved our clothes. They joined Paul and Dave to climb a mountain where a castle perched, its parapets steep and forbidding. Holy Jesus Son of God! (At Lourdes I went for religious exclamations.) We spotted them high up, scaling a towering wall, oblivious to danger, and too far away to hear us calling or for us to catch them. Dom had not allowed us to visit any castles, and the boys were determined to escape their dad and explore at least one. They sneaked in and saw it all, slipping behind guides who were conducting tours in English so they could hear the tales of yore, managing not to be detected. We wondered if we would ever see them again.

Meanwhile, 40,000 (we were told) French pilgrims had arrived to take the cure. Sophie, ten years old, got lost in the crowd. Good heavens! Had we lost five of our children in beautiful downtown Lourdes? In desperation I went to the Cathedral to pray while Dom, Elaine, and Anne dashed around searching for them. Thank you Mary Mother of God, (still trying to be appropriately devout here) there was little Sophie kneeling in a pew. She said, cheerfully, "I knew you would come here to pray for me." She was a heretic with great faith, God bless her. The boys climbed down from the castle exultant over their break-in. They said they looked both ways before they broke the law. So we did have miracles, Gracias a Dios!

Olé, Olé, Olé!

We drove out of France and into the towering, rugged Pyr-

161

enees, Basque country and our country! Cousin Alicia had a lovely big home in Burgete, Navarra, where we were to stay. Dom was born not far from her house and she showed us the very place. The ancient home still stood, the only one on the street with a yard and garden. The old, stone church where he was baptized stood nearby, whispering of sacraments, incense and generations of worship. How had it been then? Even our name was different, spelled Etxeberia, and pronounced with a rippling burr. It meant "new house."

Alicia's children were good looking and lively, and some wild card games went on among the cousins. They spoke no English, but Pete, Paul, Dave and Elaine spoke just enough Spanish to get the games rolling. They were noisy, there at the long kitchen table, as cards were slapped down and kids yelled in two languages. The home, like most Basque homes, was built over the stable where they kept their cattle and the ewes, (called lachas,) that were milked for making their famous Basque cheese. The good animal heat rose up through the floorboards to warm the house, much needed, as there was no central heating, only wood stoves. Fragrant hay was stacked in one end, delivered in ancient carts pulled by oxen. The home was immaculate. Every morning Alicia and her daughters polished the shining wood floors by wrapping their feet in towels and doing a lively dance, singing away. Years of polishing had worn them down so the wood grain rippled and the knots stood up almost high enough to stub a toe.

Anne and Elaine were in a room with a window where they gazed longingly at the soldiers standing on the corner below, handsomely uniformed in black, and topped with Spanish three-cornered hats. Spain, determined to keep the unruly Basques subjugated, had military posted everywhere, intending to quell the recent uprising against Franco. Dom was unaware of the way the girls teetered on the brink of too darned much adventure; he was so busy excitedly swapping tales and news with his relatives. I was grateful they were on the second story so they couldn't jump out. Despite a few little apprehensions, it was a grand time.

After three days, we went on to San Sebastian and checked into a fascinating hotel, Basque history seeping out of every corner. We took a day trip to Zarautz, which for me was the best part of the whole trip. Heavenly ocean, just the right temperature and perfect waves for little Joseph, small Sophie, and me lapped the shore. Further out were huge waves booming wondrously. We were warned of dangerous riptides so not even the boys were tempted to swim out too far, except for Paul, forever the adventurer. Dave was just as daring, but he seemed endowed with more sense. He didn't get in all the scrapes Paul did. Paul was caught in an undertow and could not swim out. Excitedly he told us, "The harder I swam, the farther out into the ocean I went. I was getting really scared! A BIG Basque man swam out, plowing through like a motor boat, and pulled me in!" I imagined him with a little halo and wings. Meanwhile, the rest of us dove merrily in, except Dom, who hung out on a restaurant veranda where he could watch us from afar. There was a lot to watch besides us. European ladies wore next to nothing as they sauntered about the veranda sipping delectable libations.

A Portuguese man-of-war stung Sophie and she ran screaming out of the surf. Life guards rushed to her rescue and did something that worked, plastering her little leg with whatever it was. It was
green, that's all I knew. Meanwhile, the bottom of Anne's swimsuit
was pulled down in what she thought was big waves. Then she noted
the leering faces of teenage boys, lurking close by as once again her
bottoms were pulled down. This time the perpetrator, try though he
might, could not hide. She slapped him hard and hoped to god her
father had not seen anything, because he surely would have blamed
her. What culture shock! She decided right then to marry only an
American. Holy tomatoes, what a time! But still it was a most lovely
ocean and a delectable swim. Then on we went to visit more relatives.

Cousins piled into the Ford minivan with us, eager to visit even
more cousins and to be with their American relatives, especially Dom,
whom they adored. They called him "Tio Millionario," millionaire
uncle. Their way of spontaneously bursting into song was beautiful.
Elaine, Anne and Sophie joined in as well as they could. Sadly, against
such beauty and fun they revealed a dark side. A little rabbit jumped
out of the forest and they all, even the sweet, littlest girls, yelled,
"Mátalo, Mátalo!" ("Kill it!") The lack of any wildlife, even birds, was
explained and I began to understand the violence of the Basques we
knew at home, including Dom. They are killers. As wonderful as they
can be, some of them are also capable of mindless, pointless cruelty.

When I met Dom the only thing I had heard about Basques was
the colorful story my father loved to impress our guests with. "This

Basque got his family fed and cared for and he saved his sheep through the depression playing cards in the back rooms of bars in Wickenburg. Miguel Echeverria could barely speak English, but he never lost! He was brilliant, he outfoxed everyone and came away with most of their money." What would my Dad think now that the crafty old Basque had become my father-in-law?

The homes we visited astonished our spoiled American selves. We parked in the middle of a forest on the top of a high ridge in the middle of nowhere to visit one family. Dom looked in the back of the van and whispered to me, "Count them." Goodness gracious, there were twenty cousins crammed in with our seven children. They piled out like the circus clowns who jam themselves into weird little cars. We hiked down a long hill on a trail just wide enough for an ox cart to a stone house nestled at the edge of a meadow, backed by forest. The inside, starkly plain with whitewashed rock, was so pleasingly deco-rated with family pictures and Catholic icons that it took on a lively, friendly look. A fireplace on a raised hearth burned in the middle of the dirt floor with smoke curling out a hole in the roof. A hand pump drew water up from a well. After effusive, noisy greetings the old grandmother picked up an ax and headed out the back door. "Chicken for dinner," I thought, and sure enough, she returned with some car-casses. The dinner was delicious, served on a long table with a white, linen tablecloth hand embroidered beautifully, with many of us seated up and down each side.

As primitive as their living conditions seemed, our cousins

looked just like us, even down to what they wore. They were live-ly, bright and attractive and they welcomed us into their family so warmly that we loved them. No matter the inconvenience that they rattled off Spanish so fast the children and I could not catch much of what they said. Dom had not taught us to speak Spanish. He said, "Just listen and you'll learn," quite impossible, he spoke so rapidly. We learned more from the herders. So we left Dom to revel in the rapid-fire talk with his family, and went hiking. The green meadows, bordered by thick forests, sheep and a few cattle grazing delighted us. Back at the house we feasted, laughed, hugged a lot and left.

We traveled around to perhaps twenty homes. One was over the border in France, and we had to sneak across with the relatives who were in danger of arrest as they lacked passports. They led us under fences and over barricades and we slipped silently down se-cret trails to avoid detection. How devilish! After our reunion with the French Basque relatives we trudged back up the trail. At the van, the Guardia Civil stopped us and pointed a machine gun at Dom. We were terrified, but Dom smoothly schmoozed our way out of disas-ter. How adventurous!

Our roots of old, when the Echeverrias were smugglers in those very mountains were recalled. A story about Dom's father, Miguel, fording a stream after a smuggling run, when he was just seven years old, was told with relish. Bullets splatted around him in the water as he struggled to the safety of the deep woods, but he swore he was not scared at all.

In every place we visited there were feasts and fiestas where people of all ages danced together in the plazas. One evening in Pamplona all the little cousins were to go to a fiesta in the main city plaza. "Who is going with them?" I asked. Dom translated their reply. "No need for any adult to go. In this country, anyone who even threatens women or children just disappears. No time is wasted on arrests and trials, they are just GONE, so the children are quite safe." While I was glad there was no danger, I wondered about it. No trials? No remedy for mistakes? No recourse for someone falsely accused? It was in the time of the fascist dictator Francisco Franco, El Mano Duro, (The Iron Fist), and times in Spain, especially in the Basque country, were brutal.

We visited Juan and Poli's sister Rachel's home in Urdaniz. Across the ceiling, transecting most of the house was a huge beam, stained with the smoke of ages. We asked how old the house might be, and were told, "Last year the University of Madrid came to study these ancient Basque homes. They figured that the immense beam had to have been hewn at least 700 years before Christ!"

Some of our herders who had returned to Spain hosted us also. Dom and his men rattled Spanish off excitedly, arms waving, catching up on all their news. Basilio Arregui had been one of our smartest, hardest workers, and though not a relative, he was like family. Small and wiry, quick and strong, with bright, blue eyes, he kept us laughing with his outrageous wit. Shades of George Bernard Shaw! Another culture, but the same kind of wry, acerbic barbs aimed mercilessly at any victim who happened into his world. Wine and food were served and tales were told which, for once, Dom translated for us.

The home was over eight hundred years old, as were most Basque homes in that ancient land. Built entirely of rock and stone ingeniously stacked, it was austere, yet warmly welcoming. The Basque insensitivity crept in again, painful to see. Basilio kept big ducks under his house in a dark cellar. He let them out now and then to splash in a small, tin basin. Poor ducks! I discovered another manifestation of Basque indifference to animals' needs when I admired the milk cows in their stanchions. They eagerly started licking my arms. Dom said, "They are desperate for salt." Happy to oblige, I was licked a lot.

Best of all was the time spent with Dom's mother's family in Espinal and with his dad's family in Viscaret. Grandmother Vicencia's home was on the main square in Espinal, and was a merry social center. Her brother was a funny, charming priest, Father Arcario, and many friends drifted in to visit him and to get a peek at the American relatives. Vicencia's sister kept us all happily well oiled with wine and goodies.

On we went to Viscaret. Maria and Michael, crinkled with age, laugh lines creasing their merry faces, were relatives of Grandpa Miguel's. They lived in the home that had been the Echeverria family's center for literally centuries. We were welcomed like the long-lost relatives that I guess we were. They said, in Spanish, of course, "Come! Here is the bed, made by Miguel's great grandfather, where Miguel was born." Next Maria showed us a wonderful little chair that had been Grandpa Miguel's, and gestured with lively waves of her old arms for little Joseph to sit in it, there by the big kitchen stove. They sat us all down at their long, hand hewn table and, great hosts that Basques are, fed us splendidly. Hams and big cheese wheels that hung by ropes from the rafters where they were aged to a delicious perfection were cut down and sliced up. Wine was poured, and we feasted. After a dessert of flan, the cousins, at least twenty of them, broke into song and everyone got up and danced in the long hall, whooping and hollering. Our dancing turned into a wild mix of the Basque Jota and whatever it is that American kids do. Ay, caramba, how we danced! Even Dom joined in.

Espinal was less than a kilometer from Viscaret, and the little towns shared a Pelota court where we saw a raucous game, Basque agility amazing us yet again. We thought of Grandpa Miguel playing there, back in the 1800's, where he had been a champion, good enough to make a career of it had he not chosen to emigrate to America.

A highlight for Anne and Elaine was a visit to a jailed Pelota player, a friend of a relative. Oh Fluttery heartstrings! Those crazy girls had already forgotten their decision to marry only Americans. They thought the poor young man was HOT and wanted to marry him, no matter his criminal record. Dom stepped on the gas and the girls were left with only longing and memories.

Down the Coast We Zoomed

After three weeks of visiting, struggling with Spanish, too much food and a lot of wine, as wonderful as it had been it was a relief to head for Barcelona. Admiring the fantastic Gaudi Cathedral, I looked up to its very top spire and gasped as I spotted our boys leaning out waving. They had such a high (literally) old time that when we went to see Flamenco dancers that night, they fell asleep, exhausted. "Olé!" Clap, clap, stamp, stamp! The boys and their father responded with snore, snore. But the girls and I loved it and stayed wide-awake. Little Sophie announced that she was going to become a Flamenco dancer, and indeed she did.

Bilbao was a commercial center for Basque enterprises, and we passed a huge factory complex emblazoned with "Echeverria Hermanos"—or maybe it was "Hermanos Echeverria?" We were told that so much banking, manufacturing, and shipping were controlled by Basques that resentment seethed in the Spaniards. We were greeted rather coldly when Dom chose to stay in a beautiful, upscale Spanish hotel in Zaragoza. Intuition told us that in this elegant place Basques were to be shunned. Dom secretly relished preeminence as we reveled in luxury for at least one night.

Then down the coast we careened, Dom driving. We stopped at Valencia to see a bull fight which we hated so much that when the matador was gored and carted away to an ambulance, the kids and I cheered. Dom shushed us, thumped us on our heads and tried to hurry us out before horrified Spaniards attacked us. But wait! Something was happening. The crowd turned against the matador and was booing him. We didn't know enough about bull fighting to recognize that he was awful and that he was torturing the bull with malignant anger instead of dispatching him quickly and artfully. We were right in tune to be horrified. The next day Dom spotted a newspaper headline that reported his death.

What a dreadful sport bull fighting is, cruel and dark, not only to the bull but also to the horses that were gored to death right before our eyes. The matadors of course were gorgeous in their suits of lights with their pants so tight that everything showed. All that machismo seemed over-the-top, but the bands, the music, the grand Pasa Dobles and the pageantry were beautiful.

Our next destination was Granada, down the coast. The highway was narrow and winding, carved from cliffs on one side and plunging straight down into the Mediterranean on the other. Dom drove as he always did, FAST, our tires squealing as we sped around curves. Had we gone over an edge into the Mediterranean, no one would ever know what happened to us. Just as I thought that, Dom said cheerfully, "Just think, if we went over the edge, no one would ever know what happened to us!" "What?" I thought. "For once our minds are entwined?"

On we went, admiring in quick glances the beauty of the Spanish towns and cities, often showing elegant Moorish influence. Longingly we looked at every castle and palace as we zoomed past but Dom stopped nowhere.

Speed was his way of going, and sure enough, my fear of it was justified. As he was pointing out a magnificent fig tree, he ran smack into the back of a truck. He explained to the farmer that his children had never seen a fig tree, gave him some money, and the farmer let us go. The front of our little van was only slightly bent up, and the farmer's truck was hardly dented. However, I had whiplash and when we got to our elegant hotel at Torremolinos, I had to hang my neck over the edge of the bed in agony for three days while everyone else went swimming.

Before we left, Dave cleverly managed to sneak $100 out of a hidden safe to which only Dom, Dave and I knew the combination. He loaned his brothers the money to buy some guy-type swords that they smuggled back. The thrift, the bad hotels, the prohibition on shopping did not for a minute dampen our excitement or our delight in that wondrous adventure. A good lesson for us; you can have really swell times without spending a fortune. Also, gratitude for our rough, primitive lives chasing sheep filled my heart, as living that way had given us valuable survival skills. We could create fun no matter what.

Dom was impressive, if eccentric, in the way he financed our trip. Not believing in travelers' cheques or credit cards, he carried $19,000 in cash in various pockets. When he arrived back in Colorado, five weeks later, he still had $14,000. How did he pull that off? We stayed in grade "Z" hotels except for three or four times when he longed for hot baths and put us in nice hotels with hot water.

The Cristoforo Colombo

On to Malaga! There in the harbor floated the Cristoforo Colombo, waiting to take us to New York. Tourist class was supposed to be the fun place where the young folks partied, so that is where we had made reservations. Perhaps that was true for most cruise ships but this one was for immigrants and we were down in the bottom of the ship with a lot of cockroaches, terrible food, and peasants much like the Echeverrias must have been when they emigrated. An old, Italian lady spent the trip sitting in a corner clutching bags of seeds to plant in America, her scarf wrapped around her head and her long peasant skirt tucked in to protect her. It seemed impossible that Vicencia Martinez-Erro, young and beautiful, who was to become our family matriarch, could have looked like that. How did she look? Who knew? We embraced the experience of reliving our ancestors' journey to America.

I lounged by the little pool and read Jenny Jerome Churchill's biography. I loved her for declaring, "There is much to be said for extravagance, as thrift and adventure rarely go hand in hand." (A little extravagance was to be longed for.) However, she had never experienced Wyoming, where there was plenty of adventure, a lot of it free. She had grown up in Jerome, Arizona, a mining town rough enough to have provided experiences like ours, but her father owned the whole place—which made all the difference. He sent her to England, first class, where she captured Winston Churchill's father and had Winston.

Pete, Paul and Dave shot skeet off the ship's railing, beating the socks off one player after another. Their years of shooting on the ranch were paying off. People gathered and began cheering for the young fellows. The Captain finally took them on, and was defeated, which he did not take well. He stalked off in a huff with his entourage, leaving the boys standing triumphantly among their new admirers.

Sexy? Beautiful? Snare and Delusions!

Dom took Anne to the ship's disco where an Italian rock band was playing. To his astonishment, the lead singer, with his hot, dark eyes and his passionate voice, directed all his songs straight to Anne! Dom remembered how men proffered her cigarettes and threw her air kisses as they swarmed her outside our hotel in Pamplona. He said rather triumphantly to me, "There is real hope for Anne. She's pretty sexy!" He began to treat his young daughter with a new respect, honoring her for her blossoming sex appeal. It was good that she had earned his regard after years of being passed over in favor of Elaine. However, it sent the message that to gain the approval of her dad, and of any man, sexy was the way to go. So sexy she was! Her intelligence and her integrity kept her from becoming only that. She was much more; bright, Quixotic like her sister Sophie, and with a fine sense of humor.

Dom's need to see his women as sexy and beautiful affected all of us. He would say to Elaine or me, when we were dressed up to go somewhere special, "Go do something with your hair!" Or, "Don't you have something better to wear? You look pretty fat (or too skinny!) in that." One time we were at a party in Denver with one of his handsome friends from college who was dating that year's Miss Colorado, who went on to win Miss America. She and I were wearing

174

green dresses, but hers was lovelier than mine, and no doubt about it, she was lovelier than I. Dom seemed to take that as a personal failure and he was icy cold to me, twitching and twinkling instead to Miss Colorado. But his friend liked me even better than he liked Miss Colorado, so, as was my custom, I had fun anyway.

We got the message that we had to look good or love would be withheld. The up side—always there is an up side—for Elaine, Anne, Sophie and me was that we have learned to take care of ourselves. We have never smoked (mostly) and we kept ourselves smeared with quality creams and sunscreen. Another upside that has afforded good condition was the diet Pete's doctors ordered. We adopted it, as it would have been unthinkable to let him feel separated from us in any way because of his cystic fibrosis. Low fat, low sugar, fruits, vegetables, high quality protein, no junk food, and no soda pop, how healthy! We raised our own organic meat. Dom demanded that we make everything from scratch, fresh as possible. As well as the exercise provided by working hard, we loved to hike, were famous for wild dancing, and of course, true to family tradition, we had all the fun we could stand. We were healthy, and healthy looks good.

If we slipped and looked like the dickens, which even the niftiest of us does sometimes, we realized we were still lovable. Most everyone, Dom excepted, knew that life was not all about how people looked. Some of our favorite people were physically a long way from gorgeous, but their spirits, their hearts, radiated from them more beautifully than any celebrity could manage.

I believe I succeeded in teaching my daughters that beauty is a dangerous gift. Too many beautiful people get anything they want by just standing around looking luscious, so, lacking the challenges the rest of us face, they evolve with all the depth of a saucer. Attention, yum-yums! Get off your enchanting behinds and DO something.

New York! New York!

The children and I loved being on the ocean, even low class as it was down in the lower decks with the immigrants and the cockroaches. We spent hours standing at the railing, watching the wake swish by, looking for sea life, loving the sky so clear that at night you could see into infinity. There was always the wistful, longing hope that the infinity just glimpsed in the stars would reveal Something Else. And it does, but not to eyes, only to heart and soul. The ocean seems to mirror it, as part of the Divine Dance.

While grateful for all that had been so fascinating and fun, we were glad to be back in the USA. New York looked splendid as we cruised in and disembarked at Ellis Island. Of course the kids climbed the Statue of Liberty and did not fall off. I hope our guardian angels had at least as much fun as we did on that grand trip as they surely worked hard to keep us safe.

College Bound

After Elaine's graduation from Lincoln School she enrolled in The College of Santa Fe. We thought it would be a safe place, run as it was by the Christian Brothers. She called from her dorm soon after she had moved in to ask what to do about her roommate who was falling-down-drunk. "Give her some coffee," was all I could think of. Brother Joseph, the head of the school, became one of the best friends Elaine ever had and he took care of her. He was a marvelous artist who did wood carvings, and carved two beautiful horses, Barak and Big Enough for her. They remained close friends until his death.

He did not protect her from romance. She fell for Billy Fellers, a fellow student, and no telling what would have transpired had she not left Santa Fe for Prescott College, in Arizona. It promised a better curriculum and had been founded by Chuck Kettering, of the General Motors Ketterings, who had a home on Remuda Ranch, and had grown up with us. A life-long friend, and a moving force at "PC", of course Elaine should be there. The campus was beautiful, the courses avant-garde, and Elaine began with enthusiasm.

Freshman orientation included Outward Bound tests of strength, ingenuity and ability to survive. Elaine was rappelling down a cliff when her harness broke, and she dangled upside down clinging to a single rope until she was rescued. Then, kayaking on Lake Powell, she was caught in a whirlpool, about to be swallowed, facing death, when at the last moment her guardian angel shot her out and she lived to tell the tale. Next, the students were left in isolated areas with only pocket-knives, some string and their journals for three days " to get in touch with their inner beings" or something. Elaine got in touch with the "magic of hallucination" and the "wonder of starvation." Echeverria that she was, she came out of it as glamorous as always, undaunted. There are pictures of her surviving bravely, looking gorgeous, in a travel magazine.

She left Prescott after a year, when she became engaged to Billy Fellers, and chose to spend time at home to prepare for their marriage.

Pete, meantime, had spent one semester at Orme, in Arizona. An excellent private school on a working cattle ranch, it drew the children of famous actors and those who aspired to the very best. We hoped its focus on the success of every student would give Pete what he needed to gain an education despite cystic fibrosis. He spent one of his three months there in the infirmary, and he sadly told how "The surfer brats from California" made fun of him. So he left, and was unable to even think of college as his health deteriorated.

Top: Echeverria family passport photo, 1969. Back row, left to right: Anne, Dom, the author, Paul. Front row: Joseph, Pete, Dave and Sophie. Bottom: The family returned to New York on the Cristoforo Colombo.

Top: Beautiful family home in the French Basque countryside. Bottom: The children warmly greet one of the home's residents.

180

Top: One of the French Basque relatives' old barn. Bottom: The "Little Blue Van" that transported the family through Spain.

Top: A "feast"—one of many!—with the extended Echeverria family. Bottom left: Alicia's home in Burgete.

WE LOSE OUR CAPTAIN

About twenty-five miles South of Rawlins, on the dirt road to McCarty Canyon Ranch, the rolling sagebrush flats rose up to a long ridge of low mountains. A wide band of hay meadows and grass pastureland lay at the base, with aspen and pine groves clustered here and there on the slopes. White buildings sat on the edge of a meadow, surrounded by corrals and fenced pastures. It was a beautiful place and we admired it every time we drove past. It was called Sage Creek, after the stream that meandered through it. Only about fifteen miles from McCarty Canyon, it would be a wonderful addition to our lands. Such a lovely dream it was, and then, suddenly, it came up for sale. Dom's eyes lit up with a greedy gleam.

In late February of 1970, Dom negotiated a purchase price and terms, and excitedly we looked forward to adding it to our holdings. With the 20,000 acres, the hay meadows, and meadows on top of the ridges, our need to travel so widely for range would be almost eliminated, except, of course in winter when icy Wyoming winds blew us back to Colorado.

Dom said, "Come with me to Rawlins! Keep me company." Rare were the times Dom and I could be alone together, and I was delighted that he had invited me. When we got to Rawlins, we went straight to the First Wyoming Bank and the realization swept over me that he was there to buy Sage Creek Ranch. We were ushered into a conference room and seated at a long table. Documents were stacked there, and four solemn bankers sat across from us. They were staring at me. The plot began to unfold. I was taken aback when I realized I was not invited for the pleasure of my company, but to sign over my rights to the insurance policies of which I was the beneficiary. The men twitched, obviously nervous. Were they afraid I wouldn't do it? Were they afraid I would, and would be left destitute if anything happened to Dom? No way was I going to be a victim or be pushed into anything, so I said, "If Dom died, the first thing I would do is take care of the debts and obligations. It doesn't matter in whose name the insurance benefits are." I signed. The Sage Creek Ranch was ours!

Since then, I have heard that this sort of maneuver happens to wives, and many are left in terrible straits when their husbands die or leave them. How fortunate there was property I could fall back on, and that I was a full partner in all of it, including Sage Creek Ranch, which gave me leverage. Had I not been, the water we would be in if we lost Dom would be mighty hot. (Take note, ladies. Be aware and prepare.)

On the four hour drive back to Longmont, Dom instructed me

about what to do in the event of his death. I kept saying, "Dom, you are only 44, and healthy!" He said, "Shut up and listen." He described exactly how he wanted his funeral. His family had lavish ones, with myriad clergy, monsignors and dignitaries, limousines, and wakes in the best venues, with fine wines and food. There were so many of them, and they had so many friends, these events were momentous. Dom wanted none of that. He described his coffin, simple wood, unadorned. Mass was to be said by our favorite parish priest in the little church in Wickenburg where we had been married. The wake should be pot-luck at his family's Wickenburg home. I couldn't believe I was hearing all this, but he said, "You listen, and remember!" I did.

Dewey Brown, one of his best friends who had gone through the College of Veterinary Medicine with him, told Dom that no one should have money in a safe deposit box. Should he die, the IRS would go immediately to the bank to examine the contents, holding out any negotiable assets, including cash, until probate was done. Dewy said they allow a pittance for the widow to live on, but essentially she is left nearly destitute until the estate is settled. Dom told me he had taken the $14,000 cash left over from the trip to Spain and had put it in cousin Poli's care. Should he die, Poli would bring it to me. He also left a brief case with $43,000 with Jose Mari, and told Dave, unbeknownst to me, to retrieve it if anything happened to him.

I was instructed to go to the Longmont National Bank that carried our line of credit for advice on finding a top attorney to get us through probate. He said the lady who had done our bookkeeping for years would not be adequate and that I should hire a reputable CPA firm. He had so much advice my head was spinning. I sat there in the pickup, watching beautiful Wyoming fly by, feeling unreal. There was a splendid sunset. I hoped it was God telling me "all was well, all was very well." How could Dom be thinking about death when he had just bought a gorgeous ranch?

Gradually it became clear that something was really wrong. Dom had always hated the way the herders slurped their coffee. Now he began slurping his, just slurping away, sometimes even drooling coffee down his chin. Always proud of his appearance, he became slovenly, with drifts of dandruff on his shoulders, and shirttails hanging out. He started bringing Jose Mari, Poli, Juan, and other men home with him. They shut us out, speaking only Spanish and refusing to talk to the children or me. I would ask him a question or tell him about a business matter that needed his attention, and he would turn, look at me as though he didn't know me and then turn back to his men, jabbering away in Spanish. He rarely spoke English. I had a terrible time just getting business taken care of, and I became increasingly concerned.

He developed a painful bursitis in his shoulders, and sleep was difficult. He had me massage his shoulders for hours. The passion that had brightened our lives, and had been a great part of what kept us together, was fading. Of course, I was afraid that it was my fault. Was I too old? Fat? Thin? Dom, with uncharacteristic kindness, sadly said that it was not my fault, but he would confide nothing more. Whenever a personal problem came up, mine or the children's,

186

he declared, "Only stupid idiots have problems," so there he was, stuck in his own belief, unable to ask for help beyond the massages. A storm as dark as cystic fibrosis was rumbling, shot through with lightning, threatening us. Black it was to watch a man as wonderful (when he wasn't furious) as Dom Echeverria slipping down such an ominous slope. Even darker was my fear that his "episodes" of temper, surely psychotic, would escalate into destructive violence far beyond the sheep and dogs he abused.

The Rapids in the River of Life Begin to Roar

My brothers, John and Dana, called me from Arizona. Our mother had a cripplingly bad back, and was going to two chiropractors, steadily getting worse. They could not persuade her to go to a better doctor because the chiropractors were good friends and she would not desert them. She was lying around in agony, drinking a lot. They wanted to fly her to us in Colorado, to Michael Schmid, an osteopath who had done wonders for my back. But she couldn't sit up, so she couldn't fly. They asked me to come to Wickenburg, put a mattress in the back of the station wagon, numb her with pain pills, and head for Dr. Mike in Longmont. On Spring break, the children and I headed south.

Granny Soph was house sitting for a friend out in the desert. Our arrival was merry, with celebration and reunion, despite her condition. Actually, her condition was mostly sloshed, which helped her a lot. Except the time she was driving on a dirt road, saw a poor little injured bird flapping in the dust, slammed on the brakes, and got out to save it. As she was scrambling to catch it, her dog, Woof, knocked the car out of gear and it promptly ran over her. She was dragged a short way until the car left her and swerved into a ditch. A friend drove by and was so horrified at the sight of Granny Soph lying bloody in the dirt that she didn't even stop. She just stepped on the gas to get to a phone to send help. An ambulance sped to Gran's aid and took her to the hospital.

Granny Soph enjoyed some nice pain medication and a lot of attention there. Everyone flocked to her bedside. She was loved for her warm interest in people, for her way of listening, encouraging, and dispensing wisdom. People felt safe and understood with her and she was hilarious. After four or five days enjoying celebrity (and a few drugs), she was sent home. When Joseph heard the terrible news, he asked, "What happened to the bird?" By the time we arrived, all was well, except her back and maybe the bird.

We hiked in the beautiful desert and celebrated the joy of being in Arizona, as we always had. Granny Soph's house only had room for Pete, Dave, Joe, Anne and me. Elaine and Sophie were at Uncle Pete and Aunt Billie's, and Paul stayed with the Echeverrias, drafted to help with livestock out on their desert ranches.

At 11:30 p.m., March 17, 1970, the phone rang. Granny Soph woke me up, saying, "It's Dom." I took the phone. It was not Dom. It was a sheriff calling from Kansas. He said, "Your husband has been in a fatal accident." My first thought was, "If it was fatal, that means he must have died already, or the officer wouldn't be saying fatal."

Fatal? Fatal. A stunned mind comes up with logic like that, I guess. The sheriff went on to say that his truck had slid on black ice and slammed into a bridge abutment, under an overpass, at 6:30 that evening. The time was known because his watch was smashed and had stopped. My mother said, "You always knew it was going to happen." She was right. Strange as it might seem, a feeling of profound relief swept through me. He had crashed for the last time after years of terrifying driving and sixteen serious wrecks. The terror was over.

There was nothing to be done about Dom. The man who was with him and who was driving, Jose Inchuaste, was hospitalized in Goodland, Kansas, with compound fractures of both thighs, in serious condition. He was being taken care of. Blacker clouds were gathering. Dom despised Jose Inchuaste with such a fiery hate it was incomprehensible that they would be in the same truck. There was a suspicion Dom caught him fornicating with sheep, as what else could cause such deep revulsion? Jose had arrived from Spain barely three months earlier, and did not know how to drive. He told the police, in Spanish, "The boss got sleepy, and he made me drive. I told him I didn't know how, didn't have a license, and was scared, but he pulled me into the driver's seat and told me all I had to do was just steer the truck down the highway. When we came to the curve that went under the underpass, he grabbed the steering wheel and drove us right into the pillar. I struggled to get the wheel back, but he was too strong!"

Jose Mari Artaecheverria was following, and leaped out of his truck to do what he could. He said Jose Inchuaste was in terrible shape,

189

trapped in the pickup, screaming in pain. Dom was silent. Jose Mari pulled him out and tried to get him to lie down on a snow bank, but he kept sitting up. He cried out loudly once, but then he remained silent. Jose Marie sped to a near-by farm and called for help. The ambulance and police arrived, and with great difficulty extracted Jose, administering morphine to ease his agony, got him on a gurney and into the ambulance. They placed Dom on a second gurney and put him in the ambulance with Jose. He was so calm they were not worried about him until they reached the hospital in Goodland, and realized he had died. Later, an autopsy ordered by the insurance companies revealed that had the accident happened at an emergency room entrance nothing could have been done to save him. He had been crushed from the neck down.

My poor Mom stood, wringing her hands, hoping she could help, but what could anyone do? I just wanted to go back to my room to lie down to calm my roiling stomach. In the silent dark, Dom seemed to be swirling around the room frantic and confused. He was calling to me to help him and he was trying to help me. Some Psychologists might say my sense of Dom's presence was a projection of my own confusion and desperation, but there is no doubt in my mind, in my soul, that his presence was real. I could offer nothing but prayers and to follow the directions he had so recently given me concerning his death. My digestive system went haywire and it was up and down to the bathroom all night, but other than that I felt calm, and I began to plan what had to be done.

Flights of Angels Sang Us on Our Way

(Excuse me, Shakespeare—Pretty Loose Quote)

Dom had left six ranches in Wyoming, two feedlots full of lambs, as well as bands of sheep on rented pastures across Wyoming and Colorado, fifty thousand sheep in all. Thirty-four Basque and Mexican employees had to be looked after and paid. There were seven children between the ages of seven and nineteen, two with cystic fibrosis. Deep breaths, prayer, and O.K., first things first...

Dom's brothers, Rudy and Julio, were staying at the family home in Wickenburg, planning to leave at dawn for their desert ranches to work with the livestock. I called at midnight. Rudy answered. I asked him, "Please do not go out tomorrow morning to work the sheep. I will need you. Dom has been killed. Don't wake anyone up. There is nothing that can be done till morning, and we all need our sleep to face tomorrow." He woke everyone up. Cousin Doug Pemberton woke Paul and said, "I've got something to tell you." Paul thought, "What is going on? We can't work sheep in the pitch black night." Then he realized it was something bad and he asked, "Grandma?" Doug said, "No, your Dad." Rudy brought him to Granny Soph's house. Aunt Billie woke the girls. They knew something had happened, but Billie said nothing, just brought them. They sat in a semi-circle in the little living room. All I could say was that their Dad had been killed. They went out into the desert dawn, each alone, each quiet, to face it in their own ways.

There was a huge blizzard blowing in Colorado, and Dom's

body could not be flown to Arizona, nor could we get up there. There was nothing to do but to arrange the funeral he had ordered in Wickenburg. In Longmont, our friend the mortician George Howe took care of Dom's body, and our priests and the parish community managed a memorial Mass for him. We waited days for the blizzard to clear and for his plane to arrive. He had always been late to everything, and we used to joke that he would be late to his own funeral, and now he was. Granny Soph was shocked that we could laugh at that. To help us cope, our humor got even blacker than usual.

The obligatory Rosary was held at the funeral home, crowded with relatives and friends. The children and I were to be sequestered in a crying room, but we wanted none of that. Anne borrowed her cousin Lilli's red velvet, sexy dress—one her dad never would have allowed her to wear. Since her first thought when she learned he was gone was, "Good, I am glad. Now I can be free." The outfit was her "f-k you and farewell!" She was delectably shocking. The Echeverrias were scandalized and offended, but their problems were beyond me.

I found a seat next to Dom's casket, appropriate for the widow I had suddenly become. The children gathered around too, crying room be damned. The whole thing was unreal, a nightmare. It grew worse when Dom's fierce mother, Vicencia, stormed up to me and demanded angrily, "Did you kiss him? I kissed him!" It seemed a bizarre thing to do, given my family's New England background, but I did it, as did his daughters, except Anne. She was horrified by the caked makeup the mortician had applied and said, "I'm not kissing that!" To her, and to me, it was not Dom: a chrysalis only.

The next day St. Anthony's, the little church in Wickenburg, was packed. Our good parish priest Father Gregory had flown down from Colorado to say the Mass. Dom's casket, simple cherry, stood at the foot of the altar. The seven children and I were ushered down the aisle to be seated in the front pew. Later a friend said it was amazing how courageous we all were, heads held high, eyes dry. I did not tell her we were numb. Maybe we were kind of courageous, but numb was how it felt.

After the funeral Mass, the Echeverrias took over the limousines and followed the hearse to the cemetery, leaving me to drive the children there on my own. Elaine's fiancé Billy Fellers, was shocked. He ordered me out of the driver's seat, took the wheel, and drove us to the cemetery. Billy's wonderful Texas family had raised him to be a gentleman, and he took care of us with graciousness and kindness, standing by us through the whole sad ceremony. Dom was buried next to our little son Jack.

The wake, as Dom had wished, was at his parents' home, attended by "a cast of thousands." Josie, Dom's oldest sister, confronted me angrily, in front of everyone, saying I had not honored her brother as he deserved to be honored and that it was a disgrace. She was coldly unmoved when I protested that I had done exactly as Dom wished. Some of the family did not forgive me for years. How could I have failed to provide the grand event that was Echeverria tradition? Father Gregory gathered us up and took us away, driving us out to the desert where it was quiet and beautiful, where we could feel our beloved God.

Others in the Echeverria clan generously offered to move us to Casa Grande, the family headquarters in Arizona, so they could help raise the children. I was touched, and grateful, but to lose their father, and then their home, their friends and schools, seemed too much. And then there were the sheep, the ranches, and the herders that had to be taken care of. We stayed in Colorado. Father Gregory, always a guiding and supportive friend, stuck with us.

There was a little more to it than that. With shining eyes he told me he had always wanted to leave the priesthood and marry a rich widow. My heart broke! I thought I was poor, not nearly rich enough for Gregory, and he must have someone else in mind. Years later I realized, my God, I might have been proposed to. How tragic! We would have been a great couple. He was transferred to a small parish south of Denver, we lost touch and heard later that he sank into alcoholism and died there. "If only, if only" wracked my heart. Of all the men who, in time, drifted, or lurched in and out of my life after Dom died, Gregory was the best. What might have been-----? Life seems splattered with wonderings and regrets, and there is nothing to do but embrace what is with gratitude.

A Trip to Remember, or Maybe Forget

Rudy, one of Dom's younger brothers, his wife Dolly, and a nephew, Mark, drove us back to Colorado. Gran was bedded down in

194

the back of the station wagon, drugged. The children were spread out among the three cars. Mark was blessed with an outrageous sense of humor and a hilarious collection of jokes that kept us laughing despite the circumstances.

As we passed through the San Luis Valley in southern Colorado, where we leased lettuce fields every summer, I thought we had better let the land owner know that even though Dom was gone, we would be back. I rang the doorbell at his big home. The person who answered said, "Lettuce pickers have to apply at the foreman's office. It is just down the road. You can't miss it." "WHAT?" I said, "I guess I should go comb my hair or something. I'm here to lease your whole farm." "Oh! Oh! Sorry!" Lettuce picker? I needed more than a comb. Could it have been I was showing some strain? After the recent rapids-in-our-river-of-life, I was grateful I was still standing.

Pete and Joseph were not doing well. Their breathing had become labored, and they were coughing long and hard. We checked them into the University of Colorado Medical Center when we got to Denver, and drove on. In Longmont, we took Gran straight to the Osteopathic Hospital and turned her over to Dr. Schmid. The rest of us collapsed into our home, drank some, and were profoundly grateful to Dolly, Rudy and Mark for taking care of us.

Another nephew, Mikel Echeverria, arrived soon after, along with Dom's closest brother, Roy. Mikel was a young attorney, ready to help with the legal wrangling that needed to be done. Roy stepped in to manage the livestock and the ranches.

The First National Bank of Longmont urged me to engage Tom Wood and his law firm, which I gratefully did. Tom in turn helped me to hire Tom Brock and his associates as our CPAs. We were to have our first business meeting in the bank conference room. I was scared. I felt I was just a little sheep-herding widow and that I would disgrace myself. Mikel told me, "Put on your black suit and your high heeled black boots, the same that you wore to the funeral. Arrive ten minutes late and take the seat at the head of the table. Look at the men assembled and tell yourself that you have engaged these professionals to take care of your business. Then see to it that they do." I did, and they did, for many years. What a lesson for me, who had always been first mate to Captain Dom, following his lead. Now I was captain, and the lesson Mikel taught me has served us well.

As warned, three IRS agents showed up almost immediately. Tom Wood accompanied me as we went with them into the vaults to empty the safe deposit box. Poli had just given me the $14,000, and I had it in my jacket pocket, a comforting roll of big bills. The IRS men, disappointed, found nothing they could confiscate, so we left. I felt deliciously devilish, hiding my cash from the government, and wondered what my shadow side might be. Am I an outlaw at heart? No, I chose to think of me as a tigress, fighting for my children. And yes, I "looked both ways first."

A Battle Joined

The police decreed Dom's death a suicide. The insurance

196

companies believed he had used José to kill himself to make it seem like an accident. As soon as we returned to Colorado, they laid this out, telling me that there would be no insurance benefits. I regarded their stern faces. Good God, what to do? My fierce guardian angel stepped in. With his help, I was able to convince them that Dom was a man of such honor that never, ever would he endanger another's life, and his integrity and Catholic faith would not allow him to commit suicide. I then said, "Of course José told that story. After all, he was driving illegally, killed the boss and no doubt was terrified of the consequences." A voice in the back of my head kept nagging about the times Dom said, "I'm going to kill that filthy son of a bitch!" He hated José so much I could not imagine why he was in the truck with him. I tried to get such a black thought out of my head and free myself of the suspicion that he may indeed have used miserable José to leave us.

His preparations had been so careful and his instructions were so detailed, given to me only a few weeks before, I found it very hard not to be suspicious. There were reasons he may have wanted to go. Sadly, he must have been aware that the sheep dip he had been immersed in when he was in Peru was undermining his mental capacity. He had been a ranch management consultant with President Eisenhower's Point Four Economic Development Project in Latin America, in the 1950's. An important endeavor was to address the problem of parasites in livestock, and he was to teach the Peruvians how to dip sheep. For weeks on end he stood, waist deep, in long, cement troughs, in a potent brew of sheep dip submerging each animal. We found out by chance years later the terrible consequence of such exposure. Observed in farmers, ranchers and others who worked in parasite control was a very slow but sure deterioration into insanity. Dom, a veterinarian, must have known. How terrifying for him. If he did commit suicide, it may have been a heroic act to save us all from the loss of his sanity. We will never know and it remains a mystery.

Ten days after the accident, a recall notice came from International Harvester, instructing Dom to bring his pickup in to have the Pittman Arm replaced, as it was faulty and dangerous. Our Trust officers sprang into action and searched the entire area for that Pittman Arm, envisioning a lawsuit against the truck company. It was not in the wreckage of the pickup, and even metal detectors failed to find it. Lacking any evidence, the lawsuit was abandoned. Another mystery. Perhaps it had fallen out back where it could never be found and the truck had begun to spin out of control on the curve. Perhaps Dom did indeed grab the wheel from inexperienced Jose to try to correct it.

The insurance people stood around twitching. Was I going to make them pay $615,000 in benefits? I was and I did. Thank you, Fierce Angel. José Inchauste recovered sufficiently to return to Spain, a cripple, but well provided for by our insurance.

Dom had written an excellent will back in 1959, before we had the ranches, and he had created a trust just the year before his death, but even so, it took three long, hard years before the estate was settled. We didn't know where all the sheep were at first, but we found them. A month after Dom's death someone called from Nebraska, asking,

198

"When are you going to pick up these lambs in our feed lot?" What! We retrieved them. Mysteriously, I suddenly knew things that I could not have known. Surely Dom was guiding me. There were a few lawsuits, as happens when greedy people think there is money to be grabbed, but we squashed them satisfyingly. Finally, His Honor Judge Holmes said, "Sophie, we have done all we can to settle this, but some confusion persists. If you will review and approve it we will close probate." With relief, close it we did. Still more people came forth demanding money, but we defended ourselves well. There were jackals slinking around out there.

CARRYING ON,
"DISIRREGARDLESS"

Elaine's wedding to Billy Fellers was to be celebrated right on the heels of Dom's funeral, in May of 1970. The invitations had already been mailed. St. John's was reserved, the priests eager, and the Boulder Country Club reserved for the reception. Elaine had chosen to wear my beautiful wedding gown, so long stored in tissue paper, now altered to fit her trim little body. Bridesmaids had their dresses. How could we call it off? We held a family meeting to decide if we should go ahead or cancel out of respect for Dom's death.

Dom had opposed Elaine's marriage to Billy. He thought Billy was a spoiled rich boy with all the substance of the smoke he exhaled. (Mostly pot, but we didn't know that then.) His charm cut no mustard with Dom, though the rest of us loved him for it. Finally, we decided Dom was no more, and it was Elaine's life to live as she saw fit. The wedding was on! With mischievous anticipation, we wondered what kind of party it would be when a bunch of Texans joined the wild Echeverrias.

Some of the younger Texans were evicted from the beautiful Harvest House Hotel in Boulder for running up and down the halls naked, but they pulled themselves together in time to make it to St. John's, proper as all get out. The elder Fellers were wonderful, lovely to all and gently supportive of me. We gathered at St. John's and were escorted ceremoniously to our pews, beautiful classical music filling the church, flowers radiating fragrance, the whole place packed with relatives from Texas and Arizona, as well as more friends than we knew we had.

Mendelssohn's wedding music from "A Midsummer Night's Dream" lilted through the church as the wedding party appeared. First the lovely bridesmaids: sisters, friends, and a cousin, swept in. Then came beautiful little Jennifer, spreading flower petals, with my handsome son Joseph, the ring bearer, beside her, both seven years old. They were exactly the same size, two little cousins, both of them adorable! Elaine entered on her Uncle Roy's arm, advancing in stately cadence down the aisle. She was exquisite in my satin gown trimmed with my grandmother's antique lace. Billy and his groomsmen, handsome as could be, stood waiting to greet the bride. As Fr. Gregory began the wedding Mass, Billy keeled over! Kerplop! Horrified gasps rippled through the congregation. Groomsmen and Father hauled him into the vestry. Elaine stood there on the altar, facing us, courageously calm. Or maybe as numb as we had been at Dom's funeral? There she stood, alone. I wanted to run to her, but the realization that this was her journey, not mine, held me back. She said later she wondered if it was a warning, symbolic of her future. I had the same feeling. Dom may have been right.

Billy revived, the ceremony was completed and they were married. With trumpets blaring, figuratively, the congregation and clergy caravanned to the Boulder Country Club. The Echeverrias were grieving Dom and wondering about us. They thought we must be struggling to be brave, and they tried to be comforting, but we just needed to PARTY! Most of us launched into champagne toasts, aiming for hilarity. At one point, little Sophie, just eleven, came to me and said, "Mom, Aunt Mary and Fr. Gregory were dancing and they fell down drunk right on top of me!" Saintly Aunt Mary? Father? There was no time to worry, as Aunt Josie was so sloshed she had fallen down a staircase, and people were flustering around her to see if she needed medical attention. She insisted all she needed was another drink. The Texans and some Echeverrias drove golf carts into the swimming pool when they failed to make a turn during a golf cart race. Grandma and Grandpa Echeverria sat stoically, disapproval wafting off them. The lovely Fellers and I stuffed ourselves with delectable Country Club food and "crashed" our glasses (as Elaine used to say when she was little), in many joyous, hopeful toasts. Could it have been that Elaine and Billy created a splendidly effective way to grieve? It seemed to be working.

Lurching Through the Sagebrush

The wedding was over. Our Elaine was gone. Summer came and it was time to go to the ranch. How different would it be without her, without Dom? The station wagon was loaded—six children, several dogs and a cat—and with glad hearts we headed for our beloved Wyoming. At Schwabacher's ranch, just north of Pinedale, we checked a band of sheep Juan and Poli were trailing towards the Sections, a long, low ridge of mountains we had leased. An old ewe was crippling along, and Juan mercifully loaded her in the back of the station wagon for us to take to their destination.

We needed gas and pulled into Daniel, a little town that was mostly just a gas station. The attendant, a true man of Wyoming, came out to fill us up. He peered in and a look of astonishment, eyes popping, took over his rugged old face. No wonder! The ewe had found our picnic lunch, and there she was, a loaf of French bread in her mouth, chewing away among the dogs, the cats, and the six kids. He turned and went back in the station. When he came back out he leaned in the window and gave me a white disc, saying, "Ma'am, this here's a birth control pill. Put it between yer knees and keep it there!" Well, what could I say but, "Thanks. I guess it's just what I need." And away we went.

The Quarter Circle 5 outfit had the unique distinction of using teams of draft horses to pull the sheep camps up into their National Forest grazing permits. We kept the bands on the Sections until the snow in the high country was gone and we could trail them up to the lush mountain meadows. Rugged, remote and dangerous country, as there were mountain lions and bears, it was nevertheless great for the sheep and for us, too. Beauty! Adventure!

To take care of the bear problem, Paul and two Basques, Teodoro and Simon, rigged their rifles in a triangle of trees with cords to trip the triggers when bears came to eat a sheep carcass they placed as a trap. Late at night they heard three shots in quick succession. Their plan had worked. A bear lay dead, three shots, perfectly aimed at the dead sheep, had done him in. His hide graced our floor for years.

Roy, used to the way livestock was managed in Arizona, found it too difficult. He also had trouble with the Schwabachers. He said, "I can't get along with those darned people," so we had to let the Pinedale area leases go.

Our Own Sage Creek Ranch

We had never been to Sage Creek, our new ranch. On the Fourth of July, my birthday, we headed out to explore. Past the white ranch houses and corrals was a road that led up the long range of low mountains. The station wagon was not four-wheel drive, but by golly it made it, grinding and kicking up dust, up the steep and winding road. We topped out and stared in wonder. The crest of the hill sloped down to a long swale, not quite a canyon, but a depression that caught enough ground water so that about three acres were blanketed in wild iris. A field of blue and purple flowers, so unexpected, so beautiful we let out a whoop of joy. The area past the iris stretched out to the horizon, segueing into green grass, promising happy sheep.

Back down the road we slipped and slid, winding around the bottom of the hills to an aspen grove. Most of the groves on Sage Creek

204

Ranch were mature enough to be really big, but young enough that very little dead fall had collected on the forest floors, and they were gorgeously park-like. We left the station wagon and hiked a game trail that led into a thick grove. Deep inside, suddenly there was a glade, sun streaming in, with a little brook making brook music in the middle of it. An artist might have created such a scene for a fairy tale, and there we had our picnic, in love with our new ranch.

Later we climbed to the highest point on the ranch, just above the grove we had named The Fourth of July Picnic Place. The sun was setting and clouds put on a magnificent show, lighting the land with brilliant, constantly changing reds, oranges, golds and purples, as far as we could see. Which was pretty far, all the way to Sheep Mountain, just south of Rawlins, to Miller Hill to the west, and on forever. It was going to get dark, so we scrambled down to the car and headed for home on McCarty Canyon Ranch.

Later that summer Michael and Jeannie Schmid brought their five children to visit, and we hiked Sage Creek Ranch along a stream with beaver dams that made great swimming holes. Such a beautiful day. Father Ron came to visit and we climbed the mountain just above the creek to a high point that was crowned with one lone cedar tree. We named it after him, since he had blessed it, and the entire Ranch, and us. Indeed, blessed we were.

Wheeling, Dealing, Stealing, Reeling

We had to sell three of our ranches to save the other three. Our bank trustees, attorneys, and Roy created an ingenious plan whereby we simultaneously traded Sage Creek Ranch, which I had inherited outright, for McCarty Canyon, our beloved home, which was in the Trust and vulnerable to disposition. Trusts were required by law to dispose of properties that yielded less than 1.5% of base value, and McCarty made barely enough to pay the taxes. It would have to be sold, a heart breaking possibility. We sat around a conference table and shoved papers and piles of cash back and forth to render the deal simultaneous and therefore legal. McCarty Canyon Ranch was traded for Sage Creek Ranch, which then was in the Trust. Roy immediately bought Sage Creek Ranch from the Trust, and I owned McCarty free and clear. The Trust, and Roy, made out like bandits as Sage Creek Ranch, with 20,000 acres, was twice as large as little 10,000 acre Mc-Carty Canyon Ranch, and it made good money. However, Sage Creek Ranch carried a debt, hence the auspicious sale to Roy. As was my custom, I cheerfully assumed all was well, all was very well. Our beloved home was safe.

Even so, the idea that beautiful Sage Creek would no longer be ours hurt. Since it had always been clear that we were only stewards, given the privilege of caring for the ranches as others had before us, we took it to be just that; a passing of stewardship. Now that Roy owned it, what difference would it make? We could still hike there, swim in the beaver ponds and be happy it was in the family. Sadly, another lesson was imposed. Suddenly we were made to feel like trespassers. Complaining was out, as McCarty Canyon was safely ours, the home

206

of our hearts, with more gorgeous trails to hike and places to explore than we could probably ever get to. (Eventually, we did hike over just about every spot on the place.)

There was a rumor that the Fish and Game Department wanted to buy the Siberia Ridge and Sourdough Ranches, as did Curt Rochelle, a Rawlins neighbor. I felt pretty crafty, as I instructed the Trust to play them against each other. They paid attention and the bidding was lively. A fine sale was made to Curt, and later natural gas was discovered, so all turned out well for our good friend.

I struggled to manage McCarty and the two ranches south of Wamsutter with Roy for the first six months after Dom's death. The Basque foremen would not take orders from a woman, no matter how adorably, with fluttering eyelashes, or assertively, they were issued. "Please move the fencing material by the road to the barn. It is sure to be stolen if it sits out there." I said. Nothing happened. It was stolen. Dom's and the children's guns and saddles were stolen. We knew who did it, but it would do nothing but harm to rat out relatives and friends here. Paul, Pete and Dave managed to steal most of our valuable, treasured possessions back. Many of our household goods were stolen, too. We struggled to keep it all together but we were dangerously vulnerable.

I suggested to Roy, one day, how Dom managed a problem that frequently came up. He gave me a drop-dead look that shocked the hell out of me. Apparently there was a big-brother issue between them, so I never mentioned Dom's methods, or even Dom, again. Obviously he was going to run our sheep his way, Dom and I be damned. I soon realized I needed to sell the livestock and fire those stubborn Basques. Roy bought the sheep, hired the herders, and moved his headquarters to Sage Creek Ranch.

Still, what was going on? It was difficult to work with family and some anger and resentment floated around. Roy discounted me as he had Dom. I rarely saw him, and he never consulted me about any of the issues that came up about the ranches. The Trust though kind and seemingly caring was no better. Around 1972, The trusty trustees sold the water rights on the little farm we had 30 miles north of Denver, despite my orders and then my pleas not to do it. I knew that the City of Denver was struggling for water and would in time pay us a premium. The Trust sold them for $100,000. The buyer (who shall remain unnamed here for good reason) turned around and sold them to the City of Broomfield for $500,000. Crushed and angry, I went to Wyoming and tried to forget about it.

The Basque herders, happy to be in charge of bigger and better Sage Creek, invited us to come feast with them, and feast we did. They had a record player, and Basque songs echoed through the house, inspiring a lot of wild dancing. It is an ancient custom among Basque men, when women were not available, for some to take on the feminine role and Basilio Arregui was the chosen chick. He tied a bandana around his head, sashayed around, wiggled his hips, and managed to be adorable. He danced hilariously with the men, the belle of the ball, out-shining our young ladies. We all danced in outrageous,

208

probably inappropriate, celebration. Botas were passed, streams of wine gladdened hearts and really messed up heads.

Late at night we climbed into our pickup, one of the boys driving, we girls in back, and headed for home. The cold wind braced me, stars above glittered, and I was euphoric. I stood holding on to the stock rack thinking, "Goodness gracious me! Here I am, the matriarch, in the back of a pickup, really happy, the survivor of a wild party."

But the Basques were beginning to worry me. What kind of mother was I? I did nothing to protect anyone, not even myself. Heavens above it was fun! But things were slipping off into new territory. With beautiful and wild daughters, and ambitious Bascos, I began to feel a certain hesitance about our riotous times. Their hungry looks toward the girls may have come from thoughts of glomming on to the Echeverria ranches if they could marry into the family. Or not. I could not know.

Roy was no one to turn to. He had sent his son, Little Roy, and daughter, Lilli, to us for a wonderful time on the ranches. We rarely saw him as he was too busy and then he had problems with the bank regarding Sage Creek Ranch. He was forced to sell to some Texans. He did not like cold, windy Wyoming and he left.

It was suggested (I'm kindly not telling who came up with it) that we take advantage of the government wool incentives to the tune of $98,000. It was illegal but possible if we were crafty. I needed the money, and that was quite a pile, but I am really honest, mostly, and decided I should keep my law breaking at a comfortable level, like my occasional speeding tickets. The decision earned me looks of disgust, but I was glad I had chosen not to do it. I also was grateful that I had learned not to trust so easily.

The Trust then sold 400,000 pounds of our wool for 10 cents per pound, insisting the money was needed immediately, we couldn't wait for a fair price, and the wool would deteriorate in storage. I was so confused and angry! Paul had been designated by Dom to follow him as head of our business, and wistfully I wished he were just a little older. At fifteen, he couldn't be the right hand man I so badly needed.

Steve Adams stepped in. Steve, a neighboring rancher, was surely heaven-sent. He leased the ranches, ran his cattle on them, and kept them in good shape from then on, a friend for life. Steve was a native of the Little Snake River Valley, south of our ranches, with an intriguing pioneer kind of history. He told us a story, one of many, about how his grandfather, or was it his great grandfather, and some uncles went to an auction in Denver. Baby Doe Tabor, a famous, wild, wonderful character about whom much has been written (though only we Westerners seem to know much about her), had died. She and her husband amassed huge fortunes mining silver in the Colorado Rockies. After Senator Tabor died, Baby Doe gradually lost all her money. The Adams's were there to see what treasures she had left that they might want to own. Out on a side dock, ignored or forgotten, sat Baby Doe's magnificent piano, made in Europe, gloriously hand carved. It looked lonely and abandoned, so the Adams men loaded it up, and ever since it has resided happily in a ranch house near Baggs,

Wyoming. Surely the statute of limitations has run out by now.

Steve told about a great aunt who lived on their ranch in the Little Snake River Valley. As she was riding to school one day, she fell in with a group of men heading towards Baggs, where her school was. The head rider was a charmer and teased her, trying to get her to trade horses with him. She loved her horse and turned him down flat, even though he was Butch Cassidy and his friends were The Wild Bunch. A true Wyoming woman in the making, she was elegantly unperturbed and made it to school on time.

Doc Fulton, bless his kindly heart, asked me to go with him to an Elk's Club Steak Dinner in Rawlins. It was to be a big event, and quite an honor to be invited. I accepted with delight, but I couldn't leave the children alone at the ranch. Some of the herders had been sneaking snarkily around and we were vulnerable with no one to protect us, so I told Doc I had to bring the kids along. "O.K.," he said," The Elks can set up a little table for them." I arrived with twelve, my own and their friends who were visiting. Doc never asked me out again. Darn!

My fears for the children's safety were well founded and what really went on with the herders was kept from me for years. Maybe I was spared out of kindness, or perhaps out of concern for what I might do. Who knows? Had I known, I would have joined my sons. Pete, Paul and Dave had planned to kill one of the herders. (Best to forget what he almost managed to do.) They were deadly serious, and appropriately terrified of the boys, Juan Miguel hustled the creep onto a plane for Spain, which saved his miserable life. It also saved the boys from serious trouble, though committing murder in Carbon County was not that big a deal and would likely have gone unnoticed.

Venable Barclay, Our Fearless Leader, Appears

Every springtime, the minute school was out, we left Longmont for our beloved McCarty Canyon Ranch in Wyoming. One day, Venable Barclay, a Government geologist who was doing contour maps of Carbon County and the surrounding country popped into our living room without even knocking. There he was! He knew everything about the country, its geology, a lot of its history, and he told tales of The Little Snake River Valley and the towns along its banks. Baggs, Dixon and Savery were his stamping grounds, and he had been to really wild parties there. He told of how the locals had caught a longhaired hippy, the son of some famous country singer, and had sheared him like a sheep, among other tales. He also noted, "If you ever want to 'do anyone in,' Baggs is the place, as no one notices things like that." Sage advice! Best of all, he took us into the wild places he was mapping, to mountains to climb, streams to swim in, and gorgeous forests. With Ven, we learned more about our country than even ranchers knew.

Ven also liked to party and all of us danced nights away in the Dixon Bar and ate great Mexican food in a place only the locals knew. No one cared about minors there, so there wasn't a problem with young Joseph or little Sophie. One night Joseph got so drunk he scared Ven and me, and we walked him up and down the deserted Dixon streets through the night until we were sure he was all right.

Alcohol poisoning is no joke, and little Joseph, with cystic fibrosis, was especially vulnerable. I horrified me. What kind of a mother was I anyway? Powerless, certainly. Ven seemed like the father we so badly needed and the mate I longed for, but he was married. Great friends were all we could be, good people that we were.

Ven had a home in the best part of Boulder, Colorado, and we visited him there. His wife, Laura, was lovely to us. Their three children became friends with my children who were close in age. Daughter Laurie and her mother were such ladies we made every effort to be civilized when we were with them. Ven even wore a coat and tie at home per their request. But his little daughter Anne we called "Anna The Bad Banana." She was mischief personified. In the middle of polite dinner conversation she would cheerfully interject, "How boring! Let's talk about something important like how Susie got pregnant in eighth grade!" Her sense of style was beyond most of us, with skirts too short, beads too long, and heels too high. Poor Laura!

Dulaney, Ven's son, was headed for a career in geology like his Dad. We climbed a mesa near the ranch with him and named it, "Dulaney Mesa," in memory of great times with great people.

After one glorious day of exploring, Ven took us all to the Flame, a seedy bar and club in Rawlins, for dinner. A pretty good band was playing, and Ven and I got up to dance. We had on our hiking boots, jackets, hats, gloves, scarves, the whole Wyoming thing, and Ven, heating up from our lively dance, began to take things off without missing

213

a step. My Aunt Billie had been a friend of the famous fan dancer and stripper Sally Rand, and she told me tales about her, with delicious delight. "Aha!" I thought, and removed my scarf with a flourish worthy of Sally herself and flung it away. Next my jacket, slowly, with what I fancied to be devilish sensuality. Ven's eyebrows went up and off came his sweater, obviously a prelude to something. (?) The bar crowd began to watch, and as more clothes came off and were flung away with abandon, they started to cheer us on. Sally would have been proud. The kids sat in bewildered admiration—or maybe just bewildered, and then they joined us to more cheers from the crowd. How lovely to be so celebrated in "Beautiful Downtown Rawlins." (We did not go as far as Sally did.)

Dancing at The Flame was such a success we decided to put on a dance in our barn loft. Elaine was home for a visit and it was cause for celebration. We loaded the record player with new batteries, hoisted wine, beer and goodies up, put hay bales around to sit on, if anyone ever sat, and the party was on. Gaston, Elaine's admirer du jour came, which caused big trouble! Ven had an assistant, a fine young man, Greg, who had fallen in love with Elaine, but had yet to get her to notice. In the middle of the merriment, in a fit of frustrated jealousy, Greg pushed poor Gaston out the big loft door, a good two stories up. It would surely have been his death, but one of the herders grabbed Gaston by an arm and pulled him to safety in the nick of time while another guy subdued poor Greg. Oh, elusive Emily Post, propriety just kept eluding us, but we managed to continue to have "more fun than we could stand."

214

Ven and lovely Laura eventually found their differences over elegant civility too extreme and divorced. Ven then married a fairly famous artist instead of me. I was sad. He told me later he didn't think he had a chance with me, wild woman that I was. Oh darn! I just kept missing out.

A Lovely Way to Go—But

Julian drove up to the ranch house one day and said, "We have a problem. Jesus Martinez has died. I found him sitting propped up by a fence post, frozen solid, out in the sagebrush near his sheep. He couldn't have weighed 100 pounds, and I just picked him up and sat him, frozen stiff, on the truck seat and took him to town."

Jesus was a dear old Mexican, a faithful friend of Dom's. He had told Dom that he was very old and he wanted to die out in wild Wyoming with his sheep. Dom had always given him bands close in so that he could be checked on every day. Julian found him very soon after it had happened, and there was nothing to do but to be glad for him. There was no sign of struggle or of distress, no hint of foul play, and all seemed well.

The children and I felt we should honor him, as Dom would have, so we went to his funeral. As we drove up to their home, Pete had one of his rage attacks, surely insane. (Was it because Jesus' death was looking him in the face?) He found a stick in the back of the station wagon and beat me with it, hollering obscenities. Paul and Dave got him out of the car and quieted down, but the little ceremony was ruined for us. We stood in the background, hoping no one had noticed the terrible scene. Had they? We never knew. Most likely they would not have cared as they got in a battle themselves and our effort to slip away turned into a quick escape, but not quick enough. Jesus' family suddenly turned on us and said they were going to sue us, as Dom's heirs, for leaving him alone with the sheep and causing his death. Somehow we managed to calm it all down, and it never went to court. How sad that what should have been a peaceful end for dear old Jesus ended so badly. Both Jesus and Dom were probably looking down from Heaven thinking, "Oh come off it, you idiots!"

Entertaining African Doctors

The United States Department of the Interior planned to show a group of African agronomists, all PhD's, how ranching was done in the U.S.A. We were the chosen hosts to entertain and educate them for a week, and here they came, in Forest Service trucks with rangers to oversee their instruction. Lively and attractive in a quite dark way, fluent in English, they immediately realized that the Echeverrias, especially the females, were absolutely wonderful, and we celebrated instant rapport with laughing toasts to each other and to the project. (The rangers, overshadowed, left, saying they would be back to get them.)

The tours of the ranch and the perusal of our livestock went well. They asked intelligent, PhD type questions about water, grass, breeding, lambing and calving, and they liked our answers, especially the funny ones. Their humor was as bright as ours and laughter echoed through the Canyon. There was no doubt about it, we were mutually fascinating, with cultures so different but so delightfully compatible.

The night before they were to depart, we cooked up a fine feast, put fresh batteries in our record player, and gave them a party we will remember forever. To our astonishment they displayed their sexuality so naturally, so openly, that I wondered if we would make it through the celebration without landing in some dark doctor's bedroll. We danced the night away with them, sometimes in pairs, more often as a group, following wonderfully wild steps as well as we could. As the party progressed, relief swept in as they made it clear they did not intend to take it further than sensuous dancing, distinguished men that they were.

The Department of the Interior expressed proper gratitude, even sending an impressive check. We wondered if we would ever hear from the gentlemen, but they seem to have melted back into darkest Africa.

DYSFUNCTION BLOSSOMS, OR
MAYBE EXPLODES

Dom had kept his sons' hair cut in military "butches." The Beatles were our favorites, and the boys asked, "Can we grow our hair like theirs?" I liked the shaggy Beatle manes, and said, "Go for it!" The girls, true to Basque tradition, had been diligent kitchen help, then asked, "Now can we have TV Dinners and Pizza?" (Dom had insisted on everything from scratch, fresh, no frozen and very little canned, and we baked our own bread). "ALLLL RIGHT!" I said. No longer required to work with the sheep or cook mountains of food, exciting social lives began to blossom.

Suddenly we had freedom. My brother Dana planned a river trip down the San Juan in an effort to help us heal, the summer after Dom's death. Earlier that year, *The New York Times* had done a front-page piece on Dom, as a unique "Man of the West." The reporter, Tony Ripley, had become our friend. He, his wife Anne and their three children came out from New York to join us. Our old friends from the Remuda Ranch days, the Ketterings, joyfully came along too.

218

Down the river we swished, in three big rubber rafts, Dana at the helm as our fine captain. It was glorious. We all frequently "fell out"—against Park rules—to swim in the warm water. It was a two-day trip, and Dana provided a camp and a celebration that was riotous. The San Juan won us over, and we have loved river running ever since, grabbing every chance to sail away that we could.

We were driving my Dodge Van and Dom's black and orange GMC pickup home from Vernal, Utah, where our river run ended. Cousin Roy, Paul and Anne had commandeered the pickup and were following me. When we came to the junction where we were to turn north on the dirt road that led to the ranch, the pickup did not follow. Holy headache! Those three terrifying teenagers were headed for Steamboat Springs, going about 90 miles per hour. No way would I be able to catch them, so on I went as a big thunderstorm was building. If the road got too wet, we might not make it home.

We still had a phone that summer, and a call came from the sheriff's department in Steamboat Springs. He had the three young miscreants in custody. Roy had tried to use his father's credit card to get gas and cash, and it was assumed he had stolen it, which indeed he had. They were headed for jail. The storm had made it impossible for me to drive back that night. I pleaded with the officer to put Anne, age fourteen, up in a nice motel.

Instead, she was paraded wearing nothing but her white, zip-up-the-front swim suit and a cowboy shirt for a jacket by the big cage of cat-calling criminals. They were thrilled, she was scared. Once in her cell she asked for something to read and was given three XXX novels--nothing that could be had on the ranch. She didn't sleep all night, partly due to the riveting material, and partly because her jailers spent the night peeping through the observation window to observe how she was enjoying what they had given her.

The next morning Dave and I left in the big truck, the only vehicle that could negotiate the washed-out roads, to retrieve the very bad kids. We had to leave little Sophie and Joseph in the care of Pete, a frightening prospect. I was absolutely livid at the kids, until I learned what the jailers had done. I asked Anne, "Did they give you clean sheets?" Clean sheets? Clean sheets? Well, I should have brought some kind of action against that sheriff, but I was desperate to get us out of there and home. Dave and I were so mad we made them ride all the way back on that flatbed, holding on for dear life. I followed in Dom's truck, now legally gassed up. Little Roy was returned to his dad in Arizona. Paul and Anne were grounded for the rest of the summer.

Some Friends Nobody Needs

I believed that children should be allowed to choose their own friends, and choose them they did. They veered towards the "exciting" ones, Longmont's "least socially acceptable," one might say. Chaos took over. My good Catholic friends would no longer allow their children to hang out with mine, as they had become long-haired and mini-skirted. Had my feet been in their shoes, I probably wouldn't let my children spend time with us either. One of my

220

Goddaughters recently confessed that when she was a teenager and misbehaved, her mother would say, "You are acting like those Echeverrias!" Apparently we were pariahs. Her mother told me, "I love visiting you! It gives me something to talk about for two weeks." Despite our different styles, I believe Jeannie and I really are dear friends to this day. We are both just too darned interesting not to be friends.

Dom had been so authoritarian and abusive to the children that I had leaned too far the other way to try to soften their lives. Now I tried to be both firm father and marshmallow mother, and confusion reigned. We were disgracefully out of control, and I could see why my friends were avoiding us. I was no longer invited to dinners where everyone was happily married. A nice neighbor called to tell me if ever I were lonely at night he would be glad to come over and join me in bed. Holy bed bugs! What was he thinking? Well, I knew what he was thinking, damn it, and I politely told him to go home to his wife. Our parish priest told me I was dangerous to them, now that I was a widow, and no longer was it safe to invite me to lunch at the rectory, as they had been doing happily for years.

John Black, a member of Opus Dei, a Catholic men's association so far right I couldn't see them with binoculars, knocked on my door one morning. His mission was to swear me to celibacy for life, now that I was a widow, so that I could aspire to Heaven by avoiding the degradation of (whisper-whisper) sex. I was such a lady I did not tell him to f-k off. Not that I was planning sex or anything like that, but

I was not about to close any doors. He left, a failure in his Holy mission. Good grief! Who had I become?

The Ladies' Altar and Rosary Society was one of the few places I would now be welcomed; or the Legion of Mary, where I could visit sick people, as if I didn't have enough of those of my own. It was oddly interesting, if painful, to be considered so unacceptable. One night I had a lovely dream about it. At Mass I rose from the pew and flew up past the stained glass windows, the chandeliers, and over the congregation who were looking up in awe. Around I sailed, singing, "I can fly! I can fly," like Peter Pan. Take that, you terribly nice people!

The priests and nuns, for all our unorthodox behaviors, mercifully stuck with us. They did their best to fill in as surrogate fathers, and the nuns embraced me like a sister. They invited me to their beautiful evening prayers, said in community. I thought when my children were raised I could join the convent and never be lonely again. Looking back, that is pretty hilarious, but it was a lovely thought at the time.

We must have livened their lives up considerably. I taught Catholic Doctrine to high school students for a year or so, but was fired for heresy. That an unbaptized baby, or any soul who had missed being sloshed in the Baptismal Font should be denied Heaven just did not work for me. Loudly I proclaimed that the God I loved was bigger than that and would never stoop to such picayune and cruel decrees. No, The Force loves all Creation, and will let no one slip through the cracks, even if it takes many reincarnations to get it right. Of course I was fired. I hope my students remembered some of what I so earnestly told them.

Things Change in the Church

Several of the priests ventured to McCarty Canyon to try to keep us in line. They said beautiful Masses in aspen groves, but they really preferred hiking, horseback riding, fishing and eating. For them it was high adventure. Fr. Ron slept on a bottom bunk in the boy's bunkroom. Paul, Pete and Dave, awoke one morning and spotted a furry animal crouched on the chair next to Father's bed. They grabbed their rifles, always close at hand, and took aim. Ron woke up in the nick of time, startlingly bald, and yelled, "No! No! It's my hair piece!" You might wonder about possible bullet holes in the walls. The ranch houses were riddled. Asked how I stood it, I replied, "I drank."

Back in Longmont, Dom's birthday, April 7, rolled around. We were still trying to be fairly good Catholics, though heretics, and we thought it would be appropriate to honor him by offering a birthday Mass. We chose a splendid church in Boulder, Colorado and trooped in, pious and proper as could be. The Mass began, and we knelt in prayer, hoping we would please Dom's departed spirit. It came time for communion, and the priest descended regally from the high altar, silver chalice of wine and silver bowl of holy wafers in hand, to administer the sacrament. Pete got up, stepped over the communion rail, went past the priest, up the steps to the altar, and stood behind it, the priest blessedly oblivious as he continued to give out wine-dunked wafers. Pete hoisted a carafe and cheerfully drank the rest of the consecrated wine as the congregation watched, gasping in horror. Elaine whispered desperately, "Let's get out of here! Pretend you don't know him!" Well, get out we did, followed by Pete, a devilish grin from ear to ear, pleasantly plastered.

Pete Slides Down

When Dom died, in 1970, Pete was 17. He began his ultimate slide towards death with desperation and courage. His hunger for all the life he could live in whatever time he had kept him pirouetting on the very edge, like a drunk on a beam. Between hospitalizations, fifteen different ones in his last six years, and long spells of recuperation, he was a wild man. Sometimes he was shockingly inappropriate, throwing food and taunting waitresses in restaurants, often loudly rude, without warning or provocation. Alternately, thank God, he was bright, fun and interesting, so he was able to attract friends, some of them girls.

Pete drove like a mad man. Scared us all nearly to death. Once he fell asleep and banged into a power pole, bending the hood of his truck so that it would stay shut only when he was driving fast (he said), so he sped through Longmont, ignoring stop signs. When the police stopped him, and the hood popped up, he explained the situation and, miraculously they let him go.

For Pete, suicidal thoughts came and went. A huge flume shot out of a dam in Wyoming, and across it was a narrow beam. Pete pranced out on it, weaving and wavering, unable to hear our shouts over the roar of the water. We couldn't get to him, and watched transfixed, waiting for his frail little body to crash into that roaring fall. Somehow, he always came back from those near exits.

The doctors at the University Hospital told us that his only hope for survival was an operation, a thorachotamy, during which the outside of his lung and the inner wall of his thoracic cavity would be abraded so that as they healed they would bond together, holding the lung up. Pete faced the horrible plan with his usual bravado, and ordered us to put on a "last supper," the night before surgery. Pete's doctors were apprehensive, but what was there to lose? We bought a beautiful, brown velvet jacket, a little big, so that Pete could be rigged up with tubes and bottles in various pockets that wouldn't show. We paraded out of the hospital with the staff's rueful blessings.

His Godparents, the Etchepares, came down from Cheyenne, Anne took a leave of absence from college in Santa Fe, and Elaine and Billy drove up from New Mexico. Pete's favorite people assembled at an elegant restaurant on Larimer Square. There must have been at least twenty of us, toasting him and feasting in his honor.

The surgery was successful in that he did not die. There was hope it would keep his lung at least somewhat functional. He lay in ICU on a ventilator, full of tubes, smiling. When he was taken off the machine and could talk, I asked how in the world he managed to keep smiling. He replied, "Mom, I am alive!"

Yes, our amazing Pete was alive, but a new, sad fear arose.

Would he ever be able to go back to Wyoming with its high altitude and the lack of adequate medical care?

Wyoming, African Tomatoes, Police and Romance

The Etchepares invited us to dinner in their beautiful condo in Cheyenne's Hitching Post Inn. Among their guests were Elizabeth and Jim Byrd, with whom we immediately clicked. Elizabeth was director of the Department of Education for the State of Wyoming, deeply involved with children and interested in what we were doing with the Cystic Fibrosis Foundation. Jim was the first black police chief in the United States, and Wyoming was proud yet again. Today, any position of prestige for a person of color is, blessedly, no longer an issue, but it was significant then.

Wyoming is wonderful, even if it is almost uninhabitable for many. The wind sweeps across its nearly impenetrable mountain ranges and vast expanses of what looks like nothing to out-of-staters. Winter sees temperatures drop to double digits below zero. We have Grizzly bears and wolves. No wonder our state has just barely enough citizens to qualify for a congressman. Those little matters pale in the face of the fact we were the first to grant women the right to vote, and boasted the first woman governor. Now Wyoming could boast Elizabeth and Jim! Back to McCarty Canyon we went, laughing all the way about the wonderful time we had.

Fall rolled around and we left the ranch, broken-hearted as usual. How we hated to leave that place! But Longmont was good to us, and

226

we settled in for another year of school and God only knew what else.

A Sort of Successful Garden

Paul brought me a lovely gift, three luscious African Tomato Plants. He lined them up by the big kitchen window where sun streamed in and we could all enjoy them. He was surprisingly helpful, diligently pruning them as they grew richly thick and reached for the ceiling. I kept them watered and was in love with them. Never much of a gardener, they were my pride and joy, the first plants, other than my sturdy Geraniums, that had ever thrived under my care. But I kept asking Paul, "Where are the tomatoes?" He said, "Just keep watering them, Mom. They'll produce."

Jim and Elizabeth Byrd were in town, and stopped by for a visit. Jim took one look at my precious African Tomato plants and said, "Sophie, WHAT are you doing, raising Marijuana right in your kitchen window where the whole town can see it?" "POT? Not African Tomatoes? Oh my God, WHERE is that Paul," I gasped. With broken heart, I began pushing my beautiful plants down the garbage disposal as Jim insisted I must do. Pete snatched the better part of them and spirited them away to a back corner of our yard, and replanted them behind the playhouse.

As you may know, marijuana is a bronchodilator and therefore was helpful to Pete's breathing. It also does lovely things to alleviate anxiety and pain, so we kept on growing it, though not in the kitchen window.

227

It was so helpful to Pete I was glad to grow it. He was protected from what might be had from dealers, cut with questionable stuff, and costing money. We concocted recipes; brownies, fudge, and a sandwich with garlic. Leaping Snakes! I didn't try any of it. Since the boys rarely asked for money I cheerfully assumed they were being frugal with their allowances and part-time wages, stretching them cleverly to cover ski trips and parties galore. I was so innocent! Dealing? Naaaw—.

Pot worked so well Pete decided to try LSD to see if it would help him even more. "Good God, I could SEE music!" he told us. "It was all colors; colors you cannot imagine—colors I had never seen on this earth!" It had been such a wondrous trip he did it again, but the second time was a horrible nightmare. We had a coffee table art book about Hieronymus Bosch, a medieval artist who painted nightmares and dreadful hallucinations that Pete found as fascinating as a train wreck. He said his last LSD trip was worse than old Hieronymus could ever have thought up. So that was the end of that, thank goodness. But our social lives went on riotously.

Buckingham was a park up in the foothills west of Longmont where the young people partied and mayhem went on. Scary! Always creative, I aimed to outdo Buckingham, and bought beer kegs for parties in our big back yard. The plan worked well, and I was greatly relieved that the kids were under control, or at least safer than they would be out in the woods. Hard to believe, but our local police tacitly agreed that it was better to have that rowdy crowd in our back yard, and they

228

"failed" to notice the beer kegs, (without which no one would come.) They cruised by periodically, just to check, and at about 1:00 A.M. they would suggest everyone go home.

Our police force was quite wonderful to us after Dom was killed. They took my children on a tour of their jail to impress upon them the wisdom of not getting themselves incarcerated. The kids were indeed impressed. Even so, they were so wild that I could not hire nice lady baby sitters when I went off to work for the Cystic Fibrosis Foundation or when someone was hospitalized. Off duty cops were glad to come baby-sit. I was so grateful! Years later the boys let slip that they used to give the cops beer, sit them in front of the television and go down to the basement where they misbehaved outrageously.

Surprisingly, despite our dreadful reputations, we had gathered interesting friends. Dinners and parties were held to which we invited people who were different from each other. Discussions were often deliciously heated as Republicans got into it with Democrats. Tension better described the atmosphere when we mixed our dear Jewish friends with the Catholics of our parish. Now and then we found someone really far out, a hippy or even a Basque, to liven up the scene. It was fascinating to observe how unique people can be and how they interact. We were tolerant and accepting and from that we gained wisdom. Our soirees were never boring, but word got back to us that if you were invited to the Echeverrias you were guaranteed a very good time.

Pete, following one of his surgeries, asked me to get dining

229

room chairs with padded backs to ease his pain. The only ones I could find were in a set that could not be broken up, eight padded chairs and a beautiful glass table mounted on chrome legs. The inaugural feast was a shock! We pulled up our chairs, sat down, and there, staring up at us through the glass, were our numerous dogs. They put on their doggy faces that announced that they had not been fed for weeks. Liars! How can you eat with all those faces looking up at you between the plates? Darn, we had to banish our beloved pets to the back porch, a major change in our custom.

Andy Pilkington and the Pro-Am Ski Event

Andy Pilkington was the eldest son of long-time Catholic friends and was to have become a priest, but somehow he had a little daughter (who stayed with her mother) instead. He had a reputation as a real brain, and he was handsome. In 1976, Andy appeared on our doorstep selling Shaklee, one of those products that were supposed to save our lives. He never left. It seemed he was another of those angels who have mysteriously appeared just when we needed them. Eager to be helpful, he not only showered us with Shaklee, he did things like get the car serviced and the furnace repaired. With Pete so very ill, my energy and time were devoted to him—I really needed help and there was Andy.

A Cystic Fibrosis Pro-Am ski-racing event, with parties, was scheduled in Vail, Colorado. Paul, Dave, and Andy were entered, all excellent skiers. We were to meet in Vail the night before the big races and Andy drove me up early, as I was to help with the reception. Paul and Dave couldn't get away, and were to follow later that evening just in time for the affair. A blizzard blew in, and Vail Pass was closed until the morning of the event. Paul and Dave were stuck at home.

Plans for the reception involved a lot of work and we were grateful that Andy joined us to help. We created a great party, and despite the blizzard, a good crowd made it. The band struck up and dancing began. Margaritas were passed around generously. Heavens! I heard later that they are famous for making perfectly nice ladies rather uninhibited and even passionate. No wonder the evening was such a rapturous event!

Andy had been such help that my friends quickly included him in our group. I had no date, and he filled in, dancing the night away with me, undaunted by the twenty-two year age difference. How lovely! A man who did not mind being with an "ancient crone" like me. We became very, very good friends and remained so for three years.

The next day, Paul and Dave made it over the pass and distinguished themselves by sweeping the races. They looked wonderful as they stood on the podium and were awarded their victory medals. Paul was Grand Champion, though he and Dave should have been tied. Dave's pro flubbed his run, so they came in second. The Foundation made plenty of money; we congratulated ourselves with a quick celebration and said our good-byes.

As we headed for home, we picked up a hitchhiking reporter from the event who had lost his ride because of the blizzard. Conversation was lively and fascinating about current world news. He told us the next Big Thing was going to be women with three breasts. Just what news organization did he work for anyway?

Romance Lurches In

Early in the summer, three beautiful teenaged girls rode down the ridge and into the ranch one sunny day, tied their horses to the hitching rail and knocked on our door. Holy hormones, when they met Anne and Sophie, there was such a crescendo of young minds and restless hearts it was like the Fourth of July! Could little McCarty Canyon handle such a gorgeous gathering? The men on the place would surely go up in flames. Sally, Georgie, and Katey were the daughters of Doc Johnson, a three star general, who was staying in a log cabin hidden in a canyon over the ridge from us. Their home, near Denver, designed and lavishly decorated by Doc's elegant wife, was what Wyoming folk call an "obscene edifice to ego." The Johnsons circulated in lofty social circles with important military people, Doc venerated for his distinguished career. A veteran of World War II who had experienced more than anyone should have to, General Doc was above all that and did not share his wife's desire to impress. He escaped whenever he could to hide out in wild Wyoming.

His three daughters loved to come with him. They drew water from the near-by spring, chopped wood and cooked on the wood stove. At night, they played cards by lamp light. They joyously joined the Echeverrias to hike, ride horseback, skinny dip in the beaver ponds, help with the sheep, help in the kitchen, and laugh loud and long with us. They said their mother worried. Would they be ruined in Wyoming? Probably.

Twinklingly devilishly, the young ladies shared that their poor Dad had been evicted from his wife's bed for the past fourteen years. Each had their own suites at opposite ends of their mansion. While love had gone cold, their social life remained glittering, as demanded by the elegant Beatrice, so a practical relationship and shared parenthood were maintained. The girls didn't know why their mother had grown cold. After all, Doc was a fine looking man, lithe as a tiger with a ruddy face that radiated good humor and intelligence. A thatch of grey hair topped him off handsomely. Wise beyond their years, his daughters knew that a practical relationship was not enough for a vital man like Doc. They had their eyes on me.

Equally up to no good, my daughters lamented about how their poor mother had led a life as pure as the driven snow, a languishing widow, while still so young, so alive. How tragic! The five of them conspired to bring Doc over the ridge to our ranch for food, wine and hopefully romance. Fine friendships blossomed quickly among all of us.

Doc was a great help, doing many of the things a father would have done. He helped with fences, ditches, horses, food, tools and equipment, as well as bringing us delectable goodies from City Market in Rawlins. One day a picnic was planned at their cabin, and the kids rode horseback over the ridge. I drove the long way around over a terrible road in the truck loaded with food and wine. We downed our feast, lit up with laughter, surrounded by the beauty of Wyoming, with relish. When it was time for all the kids to ride back over the ridge to spend the night at McCarty, I stayed to help Doc clean up, and he began telling me about his career.

He had been very important during World War II, consulted by presidents. In fact, he was in the Oval Office as an advisor during The Bay of Pigs crisis. The tales he told had me spellbound as I washed dishes in the old dishpan with water heated on the wood stove. We moved out to the porch, and with tin cups of wine, we watched the moon come up.

Suddenly a wild Wyoming thunderstorm boiled up. Rain came pounding down, and we huddled by the stove, waiting for it to let up so I could drive home. It didn't. We knew the road would be impassable, so there I was, stuck.

Rain pouring down, lightning flashing, thunder roaring, our affair took off! How delicious for friendship to explode into joyful passion! Years of being entirely too good for anyone's benefit washed down the draw along with the muddy storm water.

Our children were snickering loudly, quite proud of themselves for their part in getting the affair going. The summer rushed on, love lighting up our lives and delighting the kids. We were all romantics at heart and we relished outrageous behavior, so naturally it was a most happy time.

Doc liked taking good care of us, and once when a truck wouldn't start, he even drove the forty miles to Rawlins and came

234

back with a set of jumper cables, which he presented to me with pride. I thought when one was having an affair flowers or diamonds might be expected, but I was grateful for the jumper cables. Fall came and sadly we closed the ranch, they shut down the cabin, and everyone went back to Colorado.

Doc and I met discreetly now and then, usually in the safety of the mountains. He was unfailingly delightful, but I saw that it was not going to work for me. First, it grated on my version of morality. Celibate or not, he was married to a woman I knew. The kids and I had even been guests in their home. Second, he was totally unavailable. I could not call, or write, because of his wife and I saw him only at his bidding. As kindly as I could, I told him, but Generals don't take well to not getting their way and our parting was prickly.

Spring came, and we hurried back to beautiful McCarty Canyon Ranch. At dinner one night, my children asked, "Where is Doc? We really miss him." I explained the situation. Dave broke the shocked silence. "Gee, Mom, you should have held out a little longer. We really need a set of socket wrenches." So ended the General affair, in gales of laughter. If only all affairs could end that way.

Adventures with Father Harry

Fr. Harry adopted us as his own. Shortly after Dom's death, he shepherded us through our tribulations, which were many, and joined us in our adventures and hilarity, which were even greater. He took us to Santa Fe, New Mexico, to visit Elaine and her husband. Billy tried to support them dealing pot, while Elaine was back in college. They managed to get food stamps, and struggled along. Elaine rode her horse, Barak, out to streams to harvest watercress that she sold at the local Farmers' Market for a little added income. She needed a visit from us.

Out by the Race Track there was a nightclub where a great band was playing, and the kids begged to go. Father was all for it, and in we paraded, Father, Elaine, Billy, the six mostly teen-aged children, and I. The manager stopped us. He didn't want to let the minors in, but as he looked us over, he was unable to resist such a good-looking bunch. It was a splendid tribe if I do say so. He looked at Harry and asked, "Are you the father?" With nary a pause, Harry replied, "Yes, I am The Father," and we were admitted. We danced up a storm until the hippies began keeling over around us. Little Sophie, thirteen, tripped over one who was passed out on the floor, so we thought it was time to go.

Wistfully I wished Fr. Harry would leave the priesthood, marry me, and help me raise the children he loved so much. Wistfully he had thought of it, too. He told me so, out of the blue. My heart leaped, but then he explained that his education as a priest made possible only some lowly job in a bank. He could not endure the loss of prestige he enjoyed as the head priest of our large parish, and playing golf with the Archbishop in Denver.

The nuns and I went with him to a conference at El Pomar, in Colorado Springs, to advance our expertise in Catholic education. After several days of trying not to fall asleep during lectures, I was delighted when Father invited me to dinner at The Broadmoor Hotel.

236

Lots of clergy were with us and when the band began to play everyone started to dance. Father Harry asked me, and as we swanned around the floor, he began to pant ardently in my ear. Holy tomcats! I didn't know what to think, good little Catholic that I was. The next morning, as we rode back to Longmont on the parish bus, I kept feeling the hair on my neck prickle as I remembered that strange dance.

Not long after that, he soulfully, earnestly, told me he wanted to be the very finest priest possible, and that he could not accomplish that without "experiencing life." There was no wonder about that, as one of the most serious problems with the Catholic Church, (in my opinion) was how out of touch the lofty clergy were. He asked me to help him in his holy goal, so I became his mistress for three years. The experiences he gained with my fairly outrageous help were wild and wonderful for both of us. I believed I was truly doing good, obediently bowing to the vaunted wisdom of my priest, as was proper for a lowly Catholic woman.

Harry cooked up daring trysts, usually up in the mountains, sometimes in Denver or Colorado Springs. When he picked me up in his nifty Mercedes, he told me to get down on the floor so no one would see me as we drove through Longmont. That shadow side I have, the mischievous part, relished the unseemliness of it.

Father wanted to save Mexican orphans and planned a trip to investigate the possibility of working in an orphanage. I think he secretly hoped he could get me to join him on his mission, as he invited me, Pete and Joseph to go with him. We flew to Phoenix, where he rented a little Volkswagen, and away we went to Mexico. Father Harry saw himself as a man of the people, which was quite noble, as he had been raised in a wealthy family with all the privileges that went with it. He patronized the worst places he could find as we drove south. One night, I was trying to sleep in a dreadful bed in a grungy room when a racket outside woke me, terrified. It sounded like a pig being stuck—you know the old saying, "Hollered like a stuck pig"—I crept to the window to see what mayhem was taking place, and it was a pig being stuck. I put a pillow over my head, shed a tear and waited for blessed morning.

The poverty was daunting. Whatever could be done about it? Anything I could do would be so infinitesimal, it would seem kind of insulting. At Mass one morning, in one of those ornate cathedrals Catholics love, I sat beside a little, shriveled up, gray man. He was shivering, so I put my beautiful Saks Fifth Avenue cardigan around his shoulders. Then I shivered. Serves me right, I thought, for being such a rich (comparatively), dumb tourist.

The little Volkswagen was great, almost as agile as a motor-cycle on the narrow, winding roads, and Father sped along with con-fidence. Suddenly, here came the Policia! They made us get out, and they almost strip searched us as we stood beside the road, Mexicans laughing and waving as they drove by. They combed that little VW from bumper to bumper, saying that drug runners liked to disguise themselves as priests. Holy rotten bananas, were we going to end up in a Mexican jail?! Father Harry, smooth as silk, managed to get them

238

to let us go, especially since we obviously had no drugs and no money, either.

What a relief it was when we arrived at a convent in Mexico City! Father had arranged for us to be guests of the nuns, who would take us to the orphanage he was interested in. Better than a five star hotel, we settled in happily. The food, however, was austere. Nuns don't get to indulge in any pleasures of the flesh, including good eats. Despite that, they were gracious. The orphanage was wonderful, in its Mexican way. Many little folk were running about, seemingly happy and well. Sister Ignatius mentioned they had a problem with lice, so I carefully dusted us off when we got back to the convent. Father loved it and planned a future there.

But first, Acapulco. I suggested a beautiful hotel, at least for a little while. After a few lovely days, Father insisted that we move into "a hotel of the people." It was better than most we had been in, but I still was entertained by parades of cockroaches, lizards and other critters as they scurried up and down the walls. Mornings came early as cocks crowed, and people gathered up their chickens to take them swimming in the surf that broke gently in front of the hotel. "How nice! I didn't know chickens liked to surf!" I said. "Madam, they take them in to wash the lice out of their feathers."

Father had to be pried out of his noble humility. We were in Mexico, and we had to see the famously fun part, lousy chickens be darned. We made it to a gorgeous, huge, pyramid shaped hotel—I can't remember the name—and Father, Pete, Joseph and I acted as though we were guests and sauntered on through the magnificent lobby and out to the pools. Then on to the beach we went, where we commandeered an umbrella and chairs, ordered drinks and goodies, and settled in. Pete and Joseph rented horses and rode up and down the beach, but the poor horses didn't enjoy it. They apparently hadn't had anything much to eat, ever, and it is no fun to ride a suffering horse. Then we dived into the surf. The water there was deliciously warm, and the waves were perfect. We spent several days there.

On the last day, Pete swam out on a board into the surf and kept going. He was headed for Australia. I grabbed a boogie board and paddled after him as fast as I could. When I reached him, way out beyond the breakers, we kind of drifted around, talking about cabbages and kings and a world of things until he agreed to come back to shore with me. It was one of a number of times he thought of suicide. With cystic fibrosis, who could blame him?

His plan was not without reason. He had another pneumothorax, a collapsed lung, something cystics too often suffer. Father found a doctor who had no idea what was wrong, and my Spanish was inadequate to explain the illness to him. The doctor and I stumbled and mumbled until he called an ambulance to take us to the airport to head back to the USA. Father got on the phone, no mean trick in Mexico, with the nuns. They managed to get us tickets on a plane we could just make. The ambulance sped across Acapulco, sirens and lights going, which pleased Pete mightily. "Hah! We're getting our money's worth," he said, between wheezes. We left Father Harry there, looking bereft, and flew to our home-away-from-home, the University of Colorado Medical Center. Once again, Pete's courage and Dr. Cotton pulled him through.

Father Harry, home from Mexico, began to feel guilty about his holy quest to experience life more fully. Naturally, he segued to projection, trying to pin it on me, seductress that I was. (Not!) It was his idea, his quest, and I had bowed to his priestly authority. I would have none of his guilt and insisted it was time for us to be just good friends. He stalked away in a snit. I think he went back to Mexico. At least we had a good time, and his priesthood must have been enhanced with all that experience I provided. I learned as much, maybe more, than he did. I'm grateful and I'm laughing.

Spirits Rise in High Altitude

After Mexico, McCarty Canyon Ranch sounded like Heaven, and we were ready to go. Pete decided he needed to be a man of independence and chose to live in his own apartment, which was better than Wyoming with its high altitude. He found a nice little place in Longmont, not far from our home, and I helped him furnish it with pots and pans and so on. It was hard to leave him. His courage was impressive, though frightening. I admitted my powerlessness over him and cystic fibrosis. We said our good-byes and headed for the ranch.

All the hikes on the ranches were beautiful, but I needed a special one. I thought of the Castle Rocks on the west end of the ranch. A surround of cliffs sheltered a little basin filled with grass and flowers. The first time the kids and I hiked there, when we topped out over the ridge, there below us in the little basin was a herd of deer, safely hidden, grazing peacefully. We tried not to disturb them, but their big ears heard us, even silent as were, and off they bounded. We crossed to the cliffs on the other side and climbed up. Tucked on a ledge just below us was a large nest of sticks, and in it were eagle chicks! Their parents were circling, screeching in alarm, so we drew back quickly, as we did not want to disturb that magnificent family. Castle Rock seemed a magical place, one where people did not belong except for quick, respectful visits.

An inner whisper directed me to the north end of the ranch instead. I came to an aspen grove, so dense, it was almost dark, quite magical, and I relished its silent embrace. A game trail led me through it and out onto a bench that overlooked miles of wondrous Wyoming. Wild flowers surrounded me. Storm clouds, magnificent, were gathering, and there was a bird flying just beneath them. Brave bird! A little poem came to me and I scribbled it on a scrap of paper I had in my back pocket.

God, my God, to You I belong, Yours I am.
Like a bird playing on the wind,
Dancing on your wind,
My soul soars, laughing in a sky alive with sun,
Strong before dark clouds rumbling thunder.

A bird delights in the wind, hovering against it,

Climbing high, then racing down in breathtaking dive,

Then caught up again, lifted, bright against the clouds.

Swift are his glides down wind tides,

Vibrant the moments he balances,

Stilled in mid-air.

One they are, wind, bird and God,

Marvelous in their dance, their divine dance.

So flies my soul with you, my Lord

Higher and higher

Until I am one with You,

Radiant in Your radiant universe.

Then, those rumbling clouds began to rain on me, and I ran down the trail to the house. A house that was merrily chaotic with children and their friends. Of course they were all hungry. Time for a little glass of wine, and onward.

Top: Anne poses in the door of a traditional Wyoming Wagon at sheep camp. Bottom: Moving a Wyoming Wagon to higher pasture.

Top: Dave, Pete, Paul and Miguel eat dinner in a Wyoming Wagon. Bottom: Julian and Elaine working sheep on the ranch.

245

Opposite page, top: Herders, Pete and Elaine drive rams across Echo Springs Ranch. Bottom: Dom, Sophie, Pete and Elaine with little dog Mayi inspect our sheep on a leased ranch in eastern Colorado. This page: Picture from the *New York Times* article about Dom.

This page, top: Dom and Elaine prepare the sheep for shearing. Bottom: Pete holds an anxious lamb waiting for its mother to be sheared.

Opposite page, top: A shearing crew we contracted from Australia, shears away! The lambs are very worried. Bottom: Charlie, the prized Rambouillet Ram that Dom bought near Pendleton, Oregon, for $600— a small fortune! Charlie was purchased to improve the quality of our wool.

Opposite page, top: The San Juan River trip with the Ketterings and the Ripleys. The author's brother Dana arranged the trip the summer after Dom's death. Bottom: Teodoro de Fuente, Paul and Simon Bulman, with their infamous bear. The trio shot the bruin on the Schwabacher's Forest Permits, north of Pinedale, WY.

This page, top: Roy Echeverria and John Etchepare—discussing sheep no doubt—after Dom died and the author and Roy were jointly running the business. Bottom: Roy Echeverria and Paul Etchepare.

251

Opposite page, top: The author and family in their Longmont living room, after Dom's death. Back row; Paul, Pete, Anne and Dave. Front row; Elaine and Sophie. Front; young Sophie and Joseph. Bottom: Paul (L) and Dave in the long hair they grew as soon as their Dad died

This page, top: The McCarty Canyon Wild Bunch, the summer of 1970, in an Aspen grove on the ranch. Bottom: Pete in 1970.

This page, top: Sophie Dominik in the mid-seventies. Bottom: Anne, mid-seventies. (What is she thinking?)

Opposite page, top: Party at Sage Creek Ranch with the herders. The herder on the right has a bandaged head after a "dust up" with a bear. A wild party with wild people. Bottom, left: When there is a shortage of women, Basque custom demands that someone pretend to be the girl for dancing. Basilio, the chosen chick, danced with everyone. Bottom, right: Elaine and Jose Marie twirling and swirling.

255

Opposite page, top: Dave checking pasture. Bottom: Elaine preparing for her wedding to Billy Fellers. Her sister Anne helps put on her garter. Billy's sister Nancy is to the far left. "Little Sophie" stands between sisters Elaine and Anne.

This page, top: Elaine's wedding party ready to leave for St. John's Church. Bottom: Elaine and Billy Fellers at the alter, after he came to from passing out.

Opposite page, top: Sophie and beloved Father Gregory. Bottom: Granny Soph and Dave. This page: The McCarty Canyon Wild Bunch pose by the hen house. The ranch house is in the background.

AMARILLO, GOODBYE

Doc Fulton drove out to the ranch to tell me I had better get to town and call Elaine. (The ranch phone was long gone.) Her voice came over the phone plaintively, "Come and get me! What is going on here is making me physically ill. I have to come home." David, Cousin Juan and I hitched a horse trailer to the big van and took off to rescue her.

Billy Fellers, so charming and so helpful at Dom's funeral, had gone to pot. Literally. Elaine said, sadly puzzled, "He sleeps with a machine gun on our bed post, anyhow I think that is what it is, and with his pistol under his pillow. He has changed so much! I can't reach him. I think he is a drug dealer, and I'm really scared."

They had been in Amarillo for two and a half years. Billy had managed to buy a cute little home, and their life, for a while, was lovely. The society Elaine found herself in was worth writing home about, and had us all saying, "Oh my God!" When the wives of Billy's friends said, "Les go shoppin'!" they meant taking Daddy's Learjet to New York.

Elaine soon tired of such high society and found a job working in Kilgore Hospital for disturbed children. She was told, "These little patients need to run out in the wilds. Here is a shovel so you can kill rattlesnakes, now take them out for fresh air and freedom." She liked that job, and her other part time job in a high-end clothing store. By then Billy was not supporting them and she needed to earn money.

We loaded all her belongings into our van and trailer. Meanwhile, Billy's lovely parents entertained us nightly with dinner at the Country Club or at their beautiful home. They surely suspected what was happening with their son and wished, as we all did, that something could be done. They loved Elaine, and understood her need to escape. Billy understood, too, and stood around, sort of helping somewhat, but he seemed to be stoned. At least he was unfailingly pleasant.

Elaine's friend Susanne who lived across the street thickened the plot (or sickened it, as Dave commented) by dashing over and calling plaintively, "Take me too! I can't stand it another minute! I'm leaving the scum bag!" Her husband was a part of Billy's drug dealing and she did indeed need to be rescued. We squashed her in, along with her cat and several potted plants, adding new drama to the exodus.

Elaine had a little Volkswagen, ancient and scarred, which she had managed to buy for practically nothing so she could get to her two jobs. We stuffed it full, including the Buffalo head she had acquired from her uncle Dana, which stuck out of the window and appeared to be looking ahead up the highway. Dave had broken his leg when he crashed Pete's motorcycle and his crutches stuck out the other window. Drivers honked and waved, laughing as they passed us. Lovely Susanne, her cat and her plants left us in Denver. We continued on up the road to McCarty Canyon. Time on the ranch was just what Elaine needed, and she revived well.

Autumn came and back in Longmont our finances were so stressed everyone went to work. Paul found a job as a waiter, and then sous chef, in Boulder's prestigious Green Briar restaurant, which was great, as he slipped delectable steaks and goodies home to us. To save the commute, he soon transferred to the Longmont Country Club as sous chef, where Dave and Sophie were bussing tables, and Anne and Elaine were waitresses. (Joseph was too young, and I was too old, so we stayed at home.) Elaine told tales about Longmont's most prominent people; who tipped generously, who were too tight to leave even thin dimes, and which old goats pinched her derriere. Very interesting inside information. We knew who was really who around town.

The Country Club had a French chef, Pierre, who fell in love with Elaine. He had been a champion race car driver and a wrestler and was a powerhouse, radiating attractive energy. There was nothing like a hot romance to heal the wounds of her just completed divorce, so we were happy for her. He liked all of us and invited us, to our surprise, to have dinner with him, his father, several children AND, his wife! Well, slithering lizards, we didn't know what to think. A wife? She was lovely, the dinner was delicious and Pierre's father nearly fell off his chair at dinner as he tried to play footsies with me under the

262

table. A strange affair, even for us, but delightful, and, after all, they were FRENCH!

Enter Dr. "F." Therapy and More!

Dom had mercilessly denigrated Pete as a sickly weakling, heaping shame upon him, but he was crafty enough to do it when others would not see. He managed to hide most of the behavior he feared might tarnish his image, and few outside the family knew anything about his dark side. Pete hated him, and small wonder. When Dom was killed he was gloatingly glad and blew his father off as a big nothing in his life. Consequently, he felt no need to prove anything to anyone, except himself. He longed to be a man like others, and he practically killed himself to do it.

First, he demanded that he have his own apartment, away from my ministrations. Next, he managed to be hired as a janitor in Woolworths, a low end department store in downtown Longmont. The manager called one day and said, "Please stop by and take a look at Pete; I'm worried about him." I walked in the door and there was Pete, sweeping the floor slowly, breathing in gasps, his face alarmingly blue. I recognized at once that his lung had collapsed again and his life was in imminent danger. The manager helped him to the car and I sped to the hospital in Denver, where the procedures necessary to re-inflate the lung were started in the ICU. Pete pulled through again, amazing man that he was.

The Cystic Fibrosis Clinic at University Hospital found a psychiatrist for Pete. The prospect of his inevitable death, the chaos that followed the loss of his father, plus a fermenting brew of other issues, had Pete so angry and in such pain that he needed help. A lot of it. His "Shrink," as he called her, was such a strong support, so able to deal with his demons that he grew to love her and their sessions became high points in his life.

"Hmmmm, I may need a little help, too." I thought. Pete's doctors obviously agreed. (Holy façade, did it show that much?) They found a psychiatrist they hoped would be helpful in the particularly unique mess I was messing with. And so it was that I entered Dr. F's elegant office and into an experience that swept me away.

Handsome, with a mane of grey hair that gave him an aura of distinction coupled with a sort of Jungian non-conformity, Dr. F. greeted me warmly. He invited me to sink into his lovely padded (prelude to a padded cell?) chair and began a remarkable run of therapy. I desperately needed help with raising the children. He said he could do nothing about them, but he could help me, and indeed he did.

Carl Jung was his idol, which gave me hope our sessions would be good. I had read some of Jung's works and loved him for his mysticism and for pulling the rug out from under sex-obsessed, bull-headed Dr. Sigmund Freud. Alas, Dr. F. did not want to talk about Carl, or indeed about much of anything except moi. His modus operandi was to drag things out of my "basement" that I did not even know were there, and help me face dark issues. A childhood fraught with pain juxtaposed confusingly with wild fun. A marriage to a rather magnificent man who periodically had what surely were psychotic breaks. And then there was cystic fibrosis. Sometimes it was so painful that tears filled Dr. F.'s eyes. Good Heavens! Was it really that bad? I guess it was, or at least he thought so.

One day those eyes bored into me intently and Dr. F. asked why I had failed to fall in love with him. "An important part of the therapeutic process includes that kind of bonding," he said. I looked over at his wife, glaring out of her silver frame on his desk. Handsome rather than pretty, with hair pulled slickly back in a chignon, her beady eyes bored into me. I got the impression she did not agree with the therapeutic process Dr. F. hoped for. Whoops! So I replied, "If I allowed myself to fall for you, I would be spending all this expensive time twitching and twinkling in efforts to beguile you, and therapy would circle the drain." Looking back, it would have been delicious to have an affair with that handsome man, but it was not what I needed. So we continued to shovel away at the junk in my basement, and he taught me survival skills. I can still hear him saying," It is not all about you," and "detach with love," among other wise tools that were lifesaving.

Dr. F. announced one day, "Sophie, you cannot lick them (the children) so you might as well join them." Holy Celebration Party! What a concept! So that is what I set about doing, and my God, was it fun! Mostly. Rapids in the river of life kept turning up.

Another Failed Romance

Dr. Chris and Joanne Amoroso thought it would be better for

265

all of us if I had a nice man to settle me down. A date was arranged with a guy named Bill. The Amorosos, Bill and I had been contestants in a National Track and Field event, held in The University of Colorado Stadium. Race walking (which Joanne had lured me into as super exercise) was our event and Bill and Chris had won medals. Joanne won our ladies' event, and I was proud that I won third place. Actually I was relieved that I finished at all and there were only three of us in the race. Bloomin' blisters, I was out of my league. Nonetheless, the Amorosos thought Bill and I would be a fine couple and would race walk happily into the sunset together.

The date with Bill was to be a celebration of their victories and the Amorosos chose a nifty little French restaurant. Bill sat across from me and things were going well enough, but there was a large flower arrangement in the middle of the table that I couldn't see over. I had to peer around awkwardly to connect with the man Chris and Joanne hoped would change my life. Finally, I took out my handy Leatherman (a set of cleverly folded tools all ranch people carry) and whacked the stems off the flowers, lowering the arrangement enough so I could see over it. Bill never looked at me again! Chris and Joanne sat there radiating disappointment. Bill was way too wimpy for me anyway.

All Hell, of Several Sorts, Breaks Loose

The Cystic Fibrosis Foundation had scheduled an event in Denver at which I was to speak. I had such a fear of saying anything in public I could barely second a motion at a Parent-Teacher meeting, so I

266

went to Dr. F. for help. He prescribed something lovely that calmed me down (practically out of this world), and I went to bed confident the next day would be just swell.

Paul and his friend Les Thurmond left a party in Les's Porsche. They hit ninety miles per hour on a dirt road and Paul was scared. He yelled at Les, "For God's sake, slow down! You're going to kill us!" They came to a curve, the Porsche began to roll, and Paul knew death was looking him in the face. He was thrown out of the sunroof as the car went over, but it pinned him down when it rolled. Lying in agony, he thought it was the end for him, but help came. Of course he was loaded. God protects drunks, they say, so Paul was alive, but he was taken to an emergency room in alarming shape.

In the early morning hours the police called me. I threw on my beautiful big, brown bathrobe with a hood and a white rope belt, just like monks wear, and sped to the hospital. There my wonderful son lay on a gurney in the emergency room, half conscious, moaning and bleeding from "contrasions and abrusions." (Thank you, Rev. Spooner, our speech challenged ancestor.) In my state of mind, Spoonerisms were to be expected. A doctor came in and said, "There is nothing broken, but he probably has internal injuries and we will keep him until we are sure he is alright." Then he looked at me quizzically. I was suddenly aware I had little on but my monk's robe. "You are unusually calm, Mrs. Echeverria," he said. I almost said, "We monks are like that," but Paul saved me. He groaned out, "She's not calm. She's bored. This must be about the hundredth time she's been called to an emergency room." On that sad but true note I went home, still zonked by whatever Dr. F. had prescribed. Paul was released the next day, slowed down, but still the Terrible Tempered Mr. Bang. I made my speech well enough, neither bored nor zonked; grateful we had come through yet again. In case you are wondering, Les came through also.

Three days later Paul rolled a big truck loaded with corn. He nearly lost his life yet again, but, stranger than fiction, the truck landed on a Ford Bronco without damaging it or killing the driver. Another miracle. The Force surely had a hand on Paul.

If You Are a Devout Catholic You Might Be Nuts.

We often do not know what is really going on if we are stuck in some all-consuming discipline like Catholicism. Here is a sad example. Anne had two friends that she insisted were to come live in our basement, as they were homeless and destitute. Louie Telemack turned out to be a good person, struggling to get his life right. Dave Peters, moderately hunchbacked, dishonorably discharged from the Marines, was a druggy who believed he was Jesus Christ reincarnated. He was scary as hell. Both were good looking, charming, and Dave had seduced Anne into being his lover. I feared having them in our house, but Anne started in on me, knowing just which buttons to push. She quoted Jesus, "If someone knocks on your door for help, it is I," or words to that effect. (Pay back for my St. Theresa con job on her?) She laid it on thick, and I crumbled. Paul, Pete and Dave said we had to get rid of them, but they would not go, and neither would their crabs.

Anne managed to break up with Dave, whereupon he tried to commit suicide, a theatrical move that failed on all counts. Unbeknownst to us, for the next four months he stalked Anne. He sat hidden under a tree in our back yard with a shotgun, watching the house. Only later did we find out from a friend what was going on and Dave and Paul finally got rid of him. "It was not pretty," they reported.

The whole episode, exacerbated by my efforts to be as holy as the dickens, Catholic no matter what, shook me to my foundations. If only I had managed the good sense to see what was happening, and to act appropriately to protect Anne! The light crept into my muddled brain—yes, perhaps being a devout Catholic was just plain nuts.

Young Sophie Gets Demoted, Promoted, and...

Sophie was eleven when Dom died, a precious little person who should have had far more loving attention through her grieving and adjustment than I was able to give her. She was popular and her friends enfolded her in love and fun. As it turned out, they provided too darned much fun, and drugs entered her life. They called her "Stony" instead of Sophie. My brother and sister-in-law, Rudy and Dolly Echeverria, came to the rescue, and Sophie lived with them in Casa Grande long enough to escape addiction.

When she came home, Longmont High School threatened a return to wild behaviors. An alternative had to be found. Lincoln School, where Elaine and I had gone, seemed so terribly far away I could not face it. The Colorado Springs School for Girls promised all that Lincoln

269

could provide, and it was close and gorgeous. Not far from the Broadmoor Hotel, in the best part of Colorado Springs, it seemed safe, so Sophie was enrolled.

She soon reported that all the girls did drugs of some kind or other, except for three smart young ladies who became her best friends. They chewed tobacco as a sort of middle finger gesture to their classmates who were smoking pot. She thrived there, the faculty loved her, chewing tobacco and all, and she was chosen to be the exchange student destined for Argentina. All was well! For the moment...

Cheyenne

Dr. F's advice, "Join the kids since I couldn't lick them" revved into high gear. It was time for Cheyenne Frontier Days, "The Daddy of Them All" Rodeo and Wild West celebration. The annual grand event was founded in 1897 by ranchers who gathered to buy and sell livestock, fur traders as they came down out of the wilderness to market their furs, and Indian tribes who reunited for celebration. Cowboys came from far and wide to compete, testing their skills roping cattle and riding broncos and bulls. We sped to Cheyenne to share the fun.

First, the Grand Parade! There we were, seven children and I, in our Stetsons and cowboy boots, looking just fine. We sat in a row on a curbstone, feet in the gutter so we wouldn't miss anything. We were all so short we often couldn't see over people and we didn't want anyone to squeeze in front of us. Apparently, we were "noticeable." The whole parade stopped several times and someone would look down at us and say, "Hi, Sophie! Glad you are here!" We relished the "fame." Maybe they were wondering what in the world we were doing sitting on the curb like that, or perhaps they were just glad to see us out and about after Dom's death. He was really the one who was famous, well known and admired throughout the livestock industry. After the parade, we took in the rodeo, of course.

Several years later we headed for Frontier Days again and this time we tore it up! The event of the evening was a party at Cheyenne's best venue, the Hitching Post Inn. The cowboys who had competed in the Rodeo were there in all their glory. A handsome young fellow who had just won the title of World Champion Bull Rider got up on the stage to sing a song he had thought up about wicked women. The band went along with him cheerfully if raggedly. Then he turned around, pulled down his Levis and mooned the room. Holy buns! What next? A nationally famous rodeo cowboy groped the Wyoming governor's wife right in front of us, and another cowboy picked Tanya Tucker up off the stage and carried her away. Good golly Molly! Of course we drank and danced, climbing up on the tables to boogie away. I had "joined them" all right; Dr. F would be delighted.

Our Friend Ron

Johnny McPherson, our occasional attorney, threw one hell of a street party in Rawlins. The weather was perfect and moonlight lent something approaching loveliness to our raunchy little town. In the seventies, Rawlins was loose and lively with the money the workers

271

earned in the "oil patch," where they were drilling for oil and natural gas. On a muddy pickup bumper, there was a sticker that summed up what much of the population was like: "Please don't tell my Mother I'm working in the oil patch! She thinks I'm a piano player in a whore house." Johnny's party promised to be really loose and lively.

Ranchers from a hundred mile radius came. Not about to miss any fun, the kids and I put on clean Levis, boots, grabbed our Stetsons and headed for town. (Shirts, too, in case you were worried.) Johnny had invited us, especially, and took me over to meet "a very important man." Ron Brownell was financial advisor and partner to two of Wyoming's major cattle operations and was indeed a big operator. From a prominent New York City family, he had fallen in love with Wyoming and relished his adopted role of cattleman, cowboy boots and all, but the patina of New York City still stuck. Johnny introduced us, and as I extended my hand to him, my front tooth fell right into my drink with a splash. (It was stuck in kind of haphazardly, having been knocked out when my horse stumbled and threw me.) There was no reason to stop the conversation, so I fished my tooth out, put it in my shirt pocket and went on talking. Ron was quite taken with my "casual" behavior, and I thought he must be a fine fellow to be interested in a lady whose tooth fell in her drink rather than some babe with grander physical attributes. We became very good friends.

Ron and I helped found a group of about forty ranchers whose aim it was to wrest the management of wild game from the State Game and Fish Commission. We took better care of our wildlife than any government employees sitting at their desks in Cheyenne could. We also adamantly believed the ability to issue hunting licenses to people we knew instead of having them given by lottery to just anybody should have been ours. And of course we deserved the hunting license fees, after all, hunters were harvesting our wildlife on our lands. A good cause, enthusiastically pursued by our Wildlife Enhancement Coalition.

We met at watering holes across the State, from the Ferris Hotel in Rawlins to the Saratoga Inn in Saratoga, to swell places in Jackson Hole and on to The Hitching Post in Cheyenne. Riotous was what it became. We drank way too much, yes we did. Even the Governor of Wyoming got sloshed with us. Ron was pivotal and did much of the organizing. Some of our meetings were quite casual. I remember sitting propped up on a king sized bed in a hotel suite in Cheyenne with Ron and three other ranchers propped up beside me, other ranchers grouped around, for an important meeting, enjoying room service, mostly liquid. Of course the endeavor failed. Even sober, beating the government is impossible.

When Ron's son, Ran, married Kelly, I was invited and joined them for the wedding in Virginia's beautiful Shenandoah Valley. Ron's brilliant sister, Barbara, was there and we became friends for life. I visited her in New York City and met her equally brilliant life companion, Elayne Feldstein, who was a professor of English at New York University. Barbara held an important position in the New York City education system, and the ladies provided me with quite an education of my own, as well as a lot of fun.

Ron and his business associates in Washington, D.C. gathered for meetings. One distinguished gentleman was a retired CIA agent who invited us to dinner. In the privacy of his home he told us in confidence that he had been part of the group who killed Che Guevara in Bolivia. Holy black doings! I managed to remain silent, and as amazed as I was, my tooth didn't fall out. One day Ron's friends took us on their gorgeous yacht up the Chesapeake Bay to the Naval Academy Yacht Club for a luncheon that was over-the-top elegant. Ron Brownell afforded me unforgettable times in places that never would have been possible without him.

Ron was business manager and partner in Taylor Lawrence's immense cattle ranching enterprises, rivaling the King Ranches in Texas at that time. Based in Casper, Wyoming, Ron made a sort of home in a motel there while they hatched a grand scheme to get into the oil business in Nigeria. The Nigerians had cattle and grass and no idea how to manage any of it. In exchange for Wyoming expertise and help, Ron and Taylor were to gain access to Nigeria's oil. Excitement ran high. Ron said they invested some $3,000,000 in the endeavor, among other things schlepping African colleagues to Zurich to meet Ron's banking contacts. To their dismay, the Nigerians (who they believed had become trustworthy friends) cheated and deceived them until there was nothing to do but take their loss and go back to Wyoming. We learned more about Africa than we really wanted to know.

Early in our friendship, Ron and I tried to be a real couple, but it did not work for me. His father was head of the Union Bank in

New York City, and Ron, impressively educated and very smart, was the Bank's troubleshooter, sent to Hong Kong, London, and a dizzying number of far-flung places. He literally lived on airplanes, with no house, not even an apartment to call his own. He was a member of the grandly exclusive Campfire Club north of New York, and he kept clothes there, his only semblance of a home. In his long absences, aware he was not going to be around for me, I engaged in some delightful and more promising relationships, so we "graduated" to a true friendship, free of entanglement.

One of our men on McCarty got roaring drunk and went to the neighboring Grizzly Ranch, climbed in a window and tried to assault their beautiful cowgirl manager. Wyoming women are not to be messed with, and she threw him back out the window. Buzz Rendle, her boss, found Ron and told him if he did not get our man out of the county he was going to kill the SOB, or put him in jail forever. Ron grabbed the guy and spirited him off to a treatment center in Colorado. He literally saved his life and restored him to sanity.

That was not the only good Ron did for us. He guided me in a few business matters and was a wise and funny companion for the whole family. From time to time he asked if he could stay in my guest room while he did business, and of course I could not deny my old friend a port in his storms. Darn it, I couldn't get him to move on, and he cluttered up our lives by conducting business on my telephone so loudly that he drowned out our conversations. His drinking escalated until one day he called my son Joseph, who knew a great deal about alcoholism, and said, "Joseph, I am ready to get help."

I drove him to a treatment center in Sedona, Arizona, and left him on the doorstep. He said later, "I couldn't believe you just left me standing there!" He then made himself famous by shifting into business consultant mode and trying to reorganize the whole place. Disaster! But he got the message about recovery and became even more popular as he embarked on sobriety so admirably that he gained a following. He helped many people and was much loved.

Top: We are ready to leave the hospital for one of Pete's "Last Suppers." Back: Pete, Elaine, her husband Billy Fellers, young Sophie, "Old" Sophie, Dave, Paul, his lovely Marilyn, and Anne. In front, Joseph and a little person who had been dumped at the Hospital and who had lived there ever since. Bottom: Jim and Elizabeth Byrd, wonderful friends from Cheyenne. He was the police chief who broke the terrible news to me that the African tomato plants Paul had brought me were really marijuana. Elizabeth was head of the Wyoming State Schools.

This page, top: The Cystic Fibrosis Pro-Am Ski Benefit at Vail, Colorado. Paul is awarded first place; the cystic fibrosis poster girl presented him his trophy. Bottom: Dave—whose pro blew it, or he would have been tied with Paul—checks out the trophy. How proud we were!

Opposite page, top: Andy Pilkington, the author and the wondrous Monica Barela at Anne's wedding to Kim Childs. Bottom: "The General" and his wife with the author at Anne's wedding in Estes Park. Andy was rumored to be a romantic interest; the General was.

280

Opposite page, top: Pete, Soph, Joseph and Father Harry in Mexico. A remarkable adventure, but less than remarkable romance. Bottom: The author and Olivia dog in the ranch's front yard. Her truck is to the right. Father Harry's Mercedes is to the left.

This page, top: Fr. Ron (in hair piece) with the author and Barak. Bottom: Fr. Ron under the tree we later dedicated to him. The boys almost shot the toupee he's wearing.

Opposite page, top: Sophie and great friend Ron Brownell in Virginia at Ron's son Ran's wedding. The lady is one of his relatives. My goodness, that was a "fur piece" from Wyoming! Bottom: Tom Wood, our great, life-saving attorney, with Mitzi. Our kind of people! This page: Wonderful friends Paul and Hellen Etchepare in their Cheyenne home.

283

LIFE AND DEATH AND
DEATH AND LIFE

My brother John hired Pete to work for him in Monument Valley around 1975. John ran Goulding's Lodge and Trading Post on the Navajo Reservation for nine years, and he knew all the Navajos, the locals, and the history of the area. It promised to be an exciting time for Pete, and hopefully helpful to John. (The pot farm could be closed down. What a relief!) Pete took his horse, Big Enough, with him so he could ride with his cousins, Barbara, Mary and Lynnie who had their horses there, too.

John taught Pete how to do some of the office and Trading Post work, he introduced him to interesting people, and it was a fascinating time for Pete. He liked the Navajos and they appreciated the feisty little guy who was so different from the usual white man. He slipped easily into the magic of their Valley and he could sense their mystical spirits. The Navajo ghosts, called "Chindis," whirled about in the dust devils the wind whipped up and Pete regarded them with respect and wonder. He rode Big Enough out into "the Rez" and became friends with the Tribe.

Then he got sick. John took him to the Seventh Day Adventist Hospital nearby, but they did not have a clue, had never hear of cystic fibrosis, and eventually called me. "Put him on the ambulance plane and send him to Denver," was the best I could think of. He flew up off the little dirt airstrip in front of Goulding's and made it to Colorado.

Most of us met him at the airport, ready to speed him to the University Hospital, but Pete announced he wanted another "Final Feast" first. Off to one of his favorite Denver restaurants for a great lunch we went. We had to be as brave as he was, but I, for one, was scared. Would he survive until we made it to the Hospital? He was barely breathing and had obviously suffered another pneumothorax, one of six he endured before he died. He recovered, and as he did, he entertained friends, including several generous girls; sometimes more "warmly" than one could imagine someone as sick as he was could manage. It was shocking! His siblings and I raised our glasses to him, and to Dr. Cotton who once again pulled him through.

It was a month before any of us could get to Monument Valley to bring Big Enough home. When we got there, the little horse was standing off from the water tank, alone. His ribs showed, his head hung low, and it was clear that the Indian horses had bullied him and kept him from food and water. How thrilled he was to see us, whinnying and trotting up to greet us! We loaded him up, took him home and nursed him back to his frisky self. Pete was relieved and glad to be reunited with his dear friend.

Not long after that, Pete's other lung collapsed, and his doctors said that he would die if another thoracotomy was not performed. Sadly they added that there was only about a 50% chance that he would survive the surgery. I went home to get ready to face whatever was to come.

I was sitting in our lovely garden, sunshine warming body and soul, praying. Sophie had come home from Colorado Springs to be there for Pete. She sat down beside me on the grass and said, "I want to talk about life and death." I put my arm around her and said, "Okay." "I'm pregnant," she said. "Three months ago, when I came home for spring break, Dave and I went out to Union Reservoir and….and….and….,"

I choked out, "WHAT!?" Couldn't she have waited until after the surgery to add that bit of news to the brew? Then I chose to take it in the spirit in which wonderful little Soph had offered it. Death and life indeed. Pete would leave, and Sophie would bring us a new little Being. We sat in the sun, arms around each other, wondering.

Pete survived! As soon as he was out of imminent danger we held a family meeting to devise a plan for Sophie and her baby. Around we went. "What were they thinking?" someone asked. "Well, they weren't thinking!" was a reply. "Who can they live with? Not me!" was one comment. "For heaven's sake, no way could I take care of her!" someone else said. Desperation was building, and contention. Not one of us was in a position to take on a newborn in the house. Finally Dave Morgan stood up and announced, "All of you, just back off. I will marry my Sophie and take care of her and our baby." The family replied, one after another, "I'll help all I can." Dave was five years older than

286

Soph, and a competent, hard-working young man with a job on a farm. We would pull together and all would be well. Some inappropriate betting was going on as to how long the marriage would last. Six weeks or six months? (It was very good for thirty-five years and produced four great children. So there, you cold hearted, doubting bettors!)

Fate Catches Elaine on the Wings of a Wedding

In 1973, Toni Etchepare, Hellen and Paul's beautiful daughter, was to wed Bill Thomson, a prominent member of one of Wyoming's leading political families. An affair that would properly honor the very important people involved was created. The Catholic Cathedral in Cheyenne, splendidly impressive, was decked with flowers at the end of every pew. The altar became a garden with glorious flower arrangements in tall urns. The Archbishop of Wyoming, Monsignors and priests, all friends of the Etchepares who were leaders in the Catholic community, "suited up" in colorful robes. Limousines cruised up; guests disembarked and presented themselves to formally attired ushers who led them to their pews.

We parked our mud-spattered truck and station wagon down the block and trooped in, as usual, almost late. The only seats left in the packed Cathedral were in the choir loft, which made a parade down the center aisle to the stairs near the altar necessary, a little embarrassing, but we managed it with dignity.

The wedding was absolutely beautiful. I almost never cry, except sometimes in movies where it is dark, but Toni and all her atten-

287

dants were so lovely, the music so magnificent, I was moved to shed a tear. As the ceremony ended, the bride and groom swept out of the Cathedral to booming music and the cheers of all who loved them.

The post wedding celebration was an elegant sit-down dinner, with seating designated by gold-trimmed cards. I was to be with the Etchepares, an honor and a delight. The family was distributed appropriately according to age and compatibility. Elaine was the last to arrive at her assigned seat. Hellen had placed her at a table for young people from sororities and fraternities from the University of Wyoming.

She found her seat and looked at the fellow beside whom she was to sit and thought, "Good grief, what a funny looking guy! Good God, I'm going to marry him!" A psychic flash! It was Joseph John Infanger, and indeed she did marry the guy. More psychic information; Joe told Elaine later that he had watched our family parade down the church aisle, all good looking, and he had admired her as the most beautiful. The thought came, "Wow! I'm going to marry her!"

Elaine had enrolled in a nursing program in 1972. She found a part-time job doing sweat tests for cystic fibrosis under Dr. Cotton's direction. He promoted her to work at the University of Colorado Medical Center with dying patients as he recognized that she had a gift for it. She cared for them so beautifully she was loved and valued. However, her promising career came to a halt when she decided it was time to marry Joe Infanger, who wasn't so funny looking after all.

Saratoga, Wyoming was the chosen site, as it was the closest town to McCarty Canyon Ranch. The little Catholic Church was lovely and the Saratoga Inn would be fine for the reception. The girls had learned to sew, and they proudly made their dresses. Elaine's was made by Pete's dear friend, Julie, and was perfect; simple, white, and beautiful. Anne and Sophie struggled with theirs; finishing them at the very last minute, out at the ranch. They were softly flowered silk and they were lovely in them. All three wore large straw hats decked with flowers. They proceeded into the church and took their places on the altar.

Then the ceremony lurched a little out of hand. Joe's mother had bitterly opposed the marriage. Our friend Francis Bassett had asked her, when she was complaining about how awful it was, "Elaine is a lovely young woman. What is your objection?" Evelyn Infanger wailed, "Joe is too young!" Francis gulped and asked, "Well, when do you think he might be old enough?" "NEVER!" Evelyn declared. So there she sat on the groom's side of the church, crying loudly enough that the whole church could hear. Paul and Dave escorted Elaine down the aisle, Pete read something appropriate, and our Joseph served as altar boy. The four of them stood on the altar with the bride and groom and could not help laughing at poor Mrs. Infanger. The priest did his best to carry on as seriously as the sacrament demanded, but it was hard. I, bad person that I was, could not hold back laughing with my sons. Despite the "noise," crying on one side, laughter on the other, Joe and Elaine were wed and have lived happily ever after, God bless them.

Now for Something Completely Different

David Morgan was to marry young Sophie, five months pregnant. He intended to provide a home for them, admirable man that
he was. Considering the circumstances, we planned a wedding that
would be intimate, protected from possible criticism, in our beautiful back yard. Several of our friends declined our invitation, scandalized as they chose to be by her pregnancy at sixteen, so protection was
indeed called for. No matter, five of her teachers from the Colorado
Springs School drove all the way to Longmont to honor her, shining
light on Sophie so bright our unfriendly friends were obliterated. Sophie was truly loved and admired, no matter a little mis-timing on the
pregnancy bit. It was a sorry thing for those who passed harsh Catholic judgment and missed all the fun. Didn't they realize Jesus would
have been there, turning water to wine and loving us all?

Many Echeverrias came from Arizona, and Morgans arrived
from hither and yon. Roxy and Bruce Crystal supplied a string quartet
that played classical music, enhancing the beauty that surrounded us.
The ceremony began. Sophie's brother, Dave, escorted her across the
lawn to the minister who was to perform the ceremony Sophie had
written. She wore a white, satin gown that flowed beautifully around
her expanding tummy, and a matching turban that magically supplied
a dignity beyond her years. No bride was ever lovelier.

Dave Morgan radiated strength and there was no doubt he
would take fine care of Sophie and their little person-to-be. They stood
in front of our spruce trees, in the sunshine; on the magnificent Navajo

rug that Dom's brothers had given us for our wedding. The ceremony was brief, then celebration! There was plenty of food and wine, much laughter and great love.

Anne Swans On

Our "Anna Banana" read things like Nietzsche's *Thus Spake Zarathrustra* and the great Russian writers her brother Joseph loved. Small wonder she found high school intolerably boring. Her good friend Kim Childs had left Longmont to study at St. John's College in Santa Fe and encouraged her to apply. St. John's had a fascinating curriculum based on The Great Books Program that had been created by Mortimer Adler at the University of Chicago and Anne most surely would not be bored. Kim told her to apply, even though she was only a junior in Longmont High. The college accepted her based on a required entrance essay, which she asked me to read. I was astonished. How did we get such a brainy person in our "Wild Bunch"? She left for Santa Fe, much too young for such an intellectual, high-flown college, I feared. I underestimated her.

She thrived for two years, but as with many bright people, restlessness overtook her and she decided she had been over-exposed to lofty intellectualism. "I'm sick of this metaphysical dog breath," she announced, and she transferred to the University of Texas, in Austin.

Kim Childs undoubtedly precipitated her transfer, forget the metaphysical dog breath. He proposed marriage and a wedding, in October of 1977, in Estes Park, Colorado, was planned. Our favor-

291

ite folk assembled, between two hundred fifty and three hundred, dressed to the nines and ready to celebrate. Our Lady of the Mountains Catholic Church was decked with flowers. Everyone was ushered in. Then "I'm Headin' For The Last Roundup," twanged out by a cowboy singer rang through the church as Kim and his best man, in Stetsons and boots, sauntered down the aisle. Then here came the bride, beautiful in white lace with flowers in her hair, as the strains of a Peruvian dance tune rippled through the church. Beside her was Paul Etchepare, her Godfather, swaying to the music. The ceremony proceeded. They were wed.

The reception was at the venerable Stanley Hotel, and we lived up to the reputation we had gained for gloriously wild soirees. Everyone danced, champagne flowed, hugs were warm and frequent as we reunited with friends, and the police only came once, when someone drove off the side of an embankment in front of the hotel. Two young gentlemen got in a fight over "moi" on the dance floor. How delicious! Andy Pilkington was my "gentleman du jour" and defended my honor. Sort of. He was quite a bit younger than I, and a source of scandal himself since he was living with me and there was mystery about what he could possibly be doing with the widow Echeverria. No matter. It was a grand affair to be fondly remembered as Anne and Kim headed back to their beloved Austin, Texas.

Sister Ann Brown

Ann Brown, a nun who had taught my children from first

grade through eighth in St. John's School, offered a course in Catholic Church history. I signed up, confused as I was about the validity of my faith and how it had lead me to be so foolish about our unwanted boarders. Ann's intellect was dazzling, and her rendition of church history knocked my socks off, as they say.

King David's sin was not in bedding the beautiful Bathsheba, as he was only human, for goodness' sake, and a man to boot. The sin was having her husband killed. Ann kept us shocked with more history. About five hundred years after Christ's Crucifixion, the Church fathers decreed that the clergy must be celibate, not because sex, even in marriage, was a sin, but because it was a matriarchal society and old wives were inheriting Church property. Of course they had to make sex sinful to cover their agenda and defend against the greedy old widows as well as the young women who hoped to latch on to them and their church money. Women became dangerous. They strongly discouraged their flocks from reading the Bible because they might "misinterpret" it without the wise guidance of their priests. Clergy went to any and all lengths to maintain strict control over their parishioners, ostensibly to protect them from themselves as they stupidly lurched into sin. Well, on and on Ann went, till my head was spinning and I needed aspirin, or something.

By the time the course was finished, I had pretty well decided I needed to free myself from the Church. Well I knew our priests would contest everything Ann had told us, and then I would need a lot more than aspirin. Intuitively I trusted Ann's information more than the

293

hide-bound dictates of the Church proper. Ann decided she trusted what she had taught us, too, so she left the Sisterhood.

She asked me to teach her how to attract men, as she really wanted to experience LOVE. (How optimistic of her!) A delicious run of dates followed, but they all ended in woeful heaps. We discussed each one, plotting survival techniques. As a widow, I had figured out that it was best to go out with a man only if he would take me some-place I was going to go anyway, so no matter what happened with him, I would have a good time. "Have no expectations" was my next piece of wisdom, as expectations would surely bite you in the ass. We had intense and funny discussions about the whole man thing.

Suddenly Richard Leinwebber appeared! He was wonderful and they were married. They adopted three little siblings who had been so horribly abused that they required great love and wisdom, which probably only Ann with her teaching experience and Richard with his huge heart could give. Theirs was a beautiful story, more holy than a lifetime in a convent could have been. (I must add: "In my opin-ion," as there were nuns whose holiness was beyond my understand-ing and they were not to be denigrated.)

The Charismatics

Escape from the Church eluded me for a while longer. Francis and Ray Bassett were long-time friends I admired for the way they met the challenge of raising their son David who was severely autistic. They became role models as I struggled with cystic fibrosis and the chaos it caused. The way they practiced their faith was inspiring. They made sense of it, intelligent as they were, anyway as much sense as could be made. (In my uppity opinion.)

Our parish had a Charismatic Prayer group that Francis and Ray found deeply spiritual. They urged me to join, and I did, confident their judgment was sound. The group enfolded me with such love and support, wandering widow that I was, that I dived in with gratitude.

Another best friend, Brian Davis, who had been a frequent member of the "moveable feast" at our house, also belonged. Brian had painted his ceiling black and hung planets over the whole room, dangling in their proper configurations. When he turned the lights out, they glowed in the dark. My kind of friend for sure! We shared a love for the wonder of space and he watched "Star Trek," so of course I trusted his judgment. I joined despite a little trepidation about the weirdness Charismatics were reputed to embrace.

The group began speaking in tongues. People went into trances, their eyes rolled back in their heads. They rocked as they sat on the floor, moaning, and then they began to utter what sounded like real language though none of us understood it. For perhaps half an hour they went on, good old middle class Catholics. Holy "good-ole," they seemed to be in states of ecstasy! I listened, fascinated. After a time, I decided that anything the wondrous Holy Spirit had to offer, including speaking in tongues, I wanted, though I most certainly was not about to sit on the floor rolling around with my eyes up in my forehead.

One day I lay on my bed, prayed, and gave it a try. Astonishingly, I began muttering something that actually had syntax! I didn't know what it was, but it was definitely not gibberish. I kept going until suddenly my cat, Cosmo, lying beside me, stood up, his hair bristling, and began to hiss! My little dog Juniper jumped off the bed and scurried under it, whining anxiously. Well, it was damned clear whatever I was doing was not from the Holy Ghost and I had better start praying different prayers! Animals are connected to the Cosmic Consciousness, they know things way beyond us and they do not lie. When I exorcised whatever dark entity had produced my foray into talking in tongues, Cosmo and Juniper jumped up beside me, happy again.

Meanwhile, Francis announced to the group that it was all a con, and she wasn't falling for it. The leaders pounced on her, saying she was under the control of the DEVIL! Francis Bassett, one of the holiest people I knew? The Bassetts, Brian and I exited amidst accusations that we were allied with Satan himself. You just cannot tell about people. They seemed so holy, so loving. Oh well, another lesson learned.

Top: Elaine and Joe Infanger at the altar of the Catholic Church in Saratoga, Wyoming, just married. Their wedding attendants were still laughing over the "noisy" ceremony. By now, dear reader, you surely know them all? Bottom: Sophie, Elaine's bridesmaid.

Opposite page, top: Sophie and Pete share a laugh. Bottom left: Anne, Elaine's brides-maid. Bottom right: Bride "Little Sophie."

This page, top: Sixteen-year-old bride Sophie with her brother Pete. Bottom: Joseph and Dave accompany the bride across the lawn to the wedding.

Top: Cousin Jim, Dave, and friend Tom in our backyard. Bottom: David and Sophie Morgan, just married.

Top: The author, Soph and Dave, and Dave's parents Meg and Dave Sr.. Bottom: Wedding party, on the lawn in our backyard. The bride changed into her "going away" dress. Back row; Joe Infanger, Dave M., Pete, Joseph and Kim Childs, Anne's husband at that time. Front; Elaine, Sophie M., Sophie E., Paul and Anne. Lying in front are Dave's dog Olivia and Dave.

Top: Cousin "Little" Roy, who lived with us for awhile. This picture really reveals his true self—a little wacko. Dave Morgan is on the right. Bottom: Ann Brown and Richard Lienwebber with their rescued, adopted children.

Top: Friend Venable Barclay, right, talks to Kim Child at Kim and Anne's wedding reception. Bottom: Venable with the artist he married in lieu of the author.

303

Top: Anne's wedding to Kim Childs in Estes Park, Colorado. Her Godfather, Paul Etchepare and Anne ready to sashay down the aisle. On the right, bride and groom ready to sashay back up the aisle. Bottom: Anne with maid of honor, Gail, displaying their true natures.

Opposite page, top: Pete in a Navajo sweat lodge in Monument Valley. Bottom: The only vehicle available for the family's trip to the Wickenburg cemetery for Pete's burial was Uncle Pete's old Chevy pickup. Somehow it seemed just right. Left to right: Dana, Dave, Soph, Andy, Joe, Elaine and Paul. Paul, up to no good, as usual.

304

Top: Stephanie Mora, forever friend, on the ranch. She was one of Pete's very best, and most loyal friends to his end. Her mother was infamous for a Casper, WY shooting spree. Bottom: Paul, up to go good, as usual.

Opposite page, top: Andy Pilkington and Uncle Pete Fletcher. After burying Pete's ashes, we spent the day playing in Uncle Pete's pool. Bottom: Anne tosses to Elaine, Dana behind her. Back row, Dave, Kim, Joe and Andy.

Top: Dave and Andy. Bottom: The author at the pool. (She flunked water polo.)

Opposite page, top: The girls. Cousin Gigi and baby, Elaine, Anne, Soph and cousin Vicencia. Bottom: Oh, happy dog! A ranch dog relaxes in a puddle on McCarty Canyon Ranch. Dave Morgan, Little Sophie's husband, is in the background.

The author stands on a ridge, surrounded by beloved McCarty Canyon Ranch as far as the see can see.

CELEBRATION,
THEN FAREWELL

Enough of that! Off with those wild children of mine Brian Davis and I went to hear Bob Marley at the University of Denver Field House. Holy Dreadlocks and Ganja! He was absolutely wonderful and how he ROCKED the crowd he had drawn! They filled the Field House with dreadlocks, all colors, and probably ganja, though we couldn't tell, still innocent as we were. The music began and joy filled the place. The hippies emulated Bob so well we couldn't quite keep up with them. Our sheep herding selves began to feel a little out of place. Would they regard us with as much wonder as we regarded them? Would they do us harm? Hells bells and bull merde, they didn't even notice us. Bob's reggae grabbed our hearts and our feet, and the energy of the crowd was so great we got up and danced with them in the aisles. Hugs were exchanged! Friends, the short-term kind, were made. Ever since, we have collected reggae recordings, especially incomparable Bob's, and we are still dancing.

Denver's gorgeous Red Rocks Amphitheater brought the Russian Bolshoi Ballet to perform, and I scraped up enough money for good seats so we could catch that beautiful event. Beautiful it was, and we sat in awe as the Russians took the stage, set so magnificently between the red rock cliffs. Mysteriously, long robes hiding their feet, they seemed not to move at all as they glided as swiftly and smoothly as ice skaters. Then they exploded in magnificent leaps and twirls. How in the world did they do that? Their Balalaikas sang in the Colorado night so gorgeously it was like being in Russia. We thought. We had never been in Russia, but surely that is how it would be.

Our tastes were eclectic, leading us from Russian Ballet to wild Texas guys at a club in Boulder, where again the music demanded dancing in the aisles. The famous old Boulder Theater brought us raunchy performances that deliriously brought out the worst in us. From the Denver Art Museum and the Zoo, which we loved from the time the kids were very little, we were swept to The Smothers Brothers, who were just beginning their career. The Etchepares got us tickets to one of their very first performances in the basement bar of a hotel in Denver. They would be famous, we knew, as they were hilarious. The Denver Symphony and Ballet were much loved, and the girls were inspired to take lessons. Those wonderful events balanced things as we were slammed into the wild rapids that churned in our river of life. Light brightening our very souls and then mud in our faces; that was the agenda.

A National Cystic Fibrosis Convention was to be held in Phoenix. I had grown up in Arizona, and it was hoped I could be especially helpful in arranging events. Pete, who was to represent the patient population, and I flew to Phoenix. We guided the planners to places like the Biltmore Hotel that had hosted every American president since it was built. A mansion famous for being over the top in ostentation made a great home tour. Golf courses and a rodeo got people outdoors in the Arizona sunshine and The Heard Museum provided insight into Native American Culture. Meetings went well, delegates were inspired, and we were grateful, proud and happy about our success.

Pete and I boarded the plane for Denver and home. The Executive Director of the Foundation took the aisle seat next to us, and the doggondest thing happened. He began proposing marriage to me, begging me! Pete was horrified and kept saying, "Don't do it, Mom!" "No way, Pete—do not worry!" I replied. He was not my type, whatever my type might have been, and I was mystified by why he thought he might be. What in the world was going on? We had been cordial associates when we worked for the Foundation, but never had he brushed my elbow or lingeringly touched my hand (thank goodness) the way men did when they had romance in mind. And for goodness sake, at least something beguiling should come before marriage proposals! Pete, younger and wiser than I was, whispered in my ear, "Mom, the guy is gay! What better cover than a widow with seven children if he is afraid of being discovered?" "What? Gay? How can you tell?" "Mom, it is easy. Pay attention."

We made it back to Denver; one heart frustrated if not broken, mine relieved if still mystified, and Pete laughing his head off. What was it about me that landed me in such unlikely pickles with impossible men?

Adventure to the End

Pete staggered on with incredible courage. When he was 23, in spite of the threat of a seventh collapsed lung, he hopped in his little orange Ford pickup and headed for Gunnison, Colorado. He wanted to visit his brother, Paul, who was a student at Western State College there.

"Let's party!" was the call, and off they went with a herd of college kids, sloshing down booze and dancing up a storm. Pete was an impressive drummer, and began shaking the place on a pair of bongos. It was a great party, the kind Pete relished, the kind that let him be part of the wild bunch instead of a sick kid.

Sometime after midnight, one of Paul's friends grabbed him and said, "Paul, I don't think your brother is breathing!" Pete was just sitting there, staring, his hands still on the bongos, not breathing. The party flew into panic, well, as much panic as they could sustain, loaded as they were. The only doctor they could reach was a dentist. The hospital, such as it was back then, had no emergency facility. Paul called me frantically, "What can I do? I don't know what to do! I think Pete is dying, if he isn't already dead!" "Get something from the dentist to ease pain, in case Pete wakes up and needs it, get an ambulance and head home!" was all I could think of.

Pete had pleaded, the many times he had been near death, to be allowed to die at home with his family, "Not in some friggin' hospital with a bunch of doctors and nurses poking stuff in me." We were going to honor that.

The trip was a nightmare. The ambulance crew kept pumping air into Pete with a black bag, and three times during the five hour drive, they gave up, saying, "Paul, he is gone." Three times Pete suddenly gasped, fighting to breathe, to live, and so they sped on, lights and sirens going, through the black night towards the Longmont Hospital.

The young emergency doctor put him on a respirator and IV's, telling us, "It does not look good." We didn't think it looked so good either, and I called Dave, who was at the University of Colorado in Boulder. Elaine, Anne and Sophie were all in other states, too far away to come. We took turns staying with him, until suddenly he came to, looked around with recognition and something that looked like joy. The same look he had when he woke up after his second thoracotomy, in ICU at The University Hospital, on a respirator, smiling. Again he was alive! He motioned for paper and pencil, and scribbled, "Get this fuckin' tube out of my throat!" Paul stepped forward and tried to pull it out, but tracheotomy tubes have balloons at the bottom to prevent such removal. We called the young doctor and told him to remove it, but he would not, citing liability for causing death, saying, "Pete will die if I remove him from the respirator." I said, "Deflate the balloon, then leave, no one is going to say anything or do anything." He would

315

not do it, and just slipped out of the room without another word. A nurse showed Paul how to deflate the balloon and silently left too. Paul said, "Here we go, Pete, hang in here with us!" and he removed the tube and turned off the respirator. Pete gasped, struggled for air, and choked out a laugh! He was back, our wild, awful, wonderful Pete. His doctor said, "Pete can't possibly live much longer. Take him home, as he has asked."

At home, oxygen canisters were lined up in his room to provide comfort, such as it was. A good sound system was set up so he could listen to his favorite music with friends and family. His taste in music changed, and he began asking for classical, the gentler kind, and even for easy listening. His appetite went up and down, and food was a struggle. He began treasuring introspection and meditation, and we often had to tell friends "Pete's resting now, but he will be glad that you came by."

He liked going outdoors in our lovely big yard to lay on a chaise in the sun, or in the shade of the little aspen grove he had planted years ago, now a shady retreat. Most of all he loved to be put in the back of his little pickup, on a mattress, oxygen bottle hooked up, and have me drive out to the foothills in the springtime to bird watch. Our favorite place was in the foothills of the Rockies, where we had discovered a little park where no one went, so it was all our own. On one side cliffs rose, and trees; aspens, spruce and pine surrounded the rest of the small meadow. The St. Vrain River rushed through, bordered by huge old cottonwoods, "Sacred Rustling Trees," as the

Hopis called them. They were home to great celebrations of courting and nesting birds.

Pete liked Cheetos and Coke, despite, or maybe because of, how unhealthy they were, and part of our trip was a stop at a small store in Lyons, to stock up on goodies. We parked the truck in the shade, and there we sat, chomping and slurping, relishing the beauty that embraced us. We reminisced about our family and our lives, the wondrous and the dark. There was plenty to laugh about, but some memories and observations left us sitting silent, escaping to the comfort of Cheetos and Coke.

Pete was a great reader, and we had profound ideas to kick around. Who was God? What about dying? What really happens when you are finally dead? Pete's mysticism, and mine, blessed us with a sure knowledge, more than just a belief, that whatever comes next is Grand. Wondrous Beings, some of them souls we know, will enfold us in love and will help us through the review that is said to take place. We will be given a fast look at all we did and what we learned as we negotiated the "very important seminar" that our stay on Earth was.

The fiery hell we read about in Dante's Inferno and that the Church described was not to be feared. We were sure it was just a construct created to scare all us stupid peasants into good behavior. Hell really would be the recognition of harm we had done and pain we had caused, unaware and unintended. Of course if we had intended to harm or hurt, our hell would indeed be hellish. We pondered that. Were we deluded in thinking that we really, truly had intended no harm? Pete's temper, his explosions, had been about his intolerable pain, surely to be forgiven, not punished. He had been punished enough already.

Whatever hell we had to face, it would not last long. Our angels, guides, relatives, whomever we were "to merrily meet" (as St. Thomas Moore said), could hardly wait to get us "upstairs" for celebration! For four months we did this, making the very best of the time we knew could end any moment.

Pete ordered me not to let him be embalmed. "My body has been cut on so often, I can't stand the thought of them sticking another knife in me. Just put me in the trunk of your car—don't even call the fuckin' undertaker—get out of Colorado in the black of night, take me to Wickenburg and stick me in the ground next to my little brother Jack, just as I am." He thought about it some more, and added, "And I don't want any friggin' Mass said, no religious crap. Have a big old party in the back yard, with plenty of booze and a lot of good food, and all our best friends. And, Mom, you shouldn't have to pay for it, so make it pot luck. Have music. Drink to me! Dance for me!"

He wrote a poem about it:

> When I die
> Remember that
> I love you
> I love you
> I love you

Don't forget me
Pray for me in a quiet church
Or in the woods
Then join your friends
And drink to me, drink to me
Drink to me
With all of your heart!

There was no way we would not honor Pete's wishes for a celebration. But...

It was against the law to take a body across state lines without first embalming it. It was also illegal to bury, or otherwise dispose of a body without having the services of an undertaker and a coffin. Even if one was to be cremated, the body had to be transported to the crematorium in a coffin of some kind. How could all that be avoided, as Pete demanded?

Lurid scenarios woke me in the middle of the night. Suppose I was driving south to Arizona with Pete's body, I was found out, and the police roared up behind us, lights flashing, guns drawn. They would open the trunk and discover poor Pete, take him off to be embalmed in Raton, N.M. and throw me in jail with a bunch of drug addicts and prostitutes. They would impound the car, put my children in foster care, and our pets in the pound. Of course I couldn't talk to Pete about it. It would be unthinkable to question his stated desire.

Finally I went to our good friend, Longmont's mortician,

George Howe, and explained the whole thing to him. He begged me not to try to escape with Pete over any state line. "Sophie, you would get in such horrible trouble—there is no way it could be kept secret. Everyone knows you; everyone is standing ready to help you. You have to accommodate what is necessary with what Pete wants. Has cremation been considered?" I said, "I haven't, and neither has Pete." George said, "Don't mention it. Go ahead and promise that you will not allow him to be embalmed and then change the subject. Don't allow a chance for him to reject cremation. It is perhaps dishonest, but it will solve your very sad dilemma." I thought about it, and agreed.

Pete's siblings agreed, too, and came up with a wonderful plan to plant Pete's ashes with a potted Norfolk Pine tree, to keep him growing with us. He would continue to live through it, sitting in our living room, part of the family still.

George rejected our plan, telling me, "Sophie, it is important to grieve fully when we suffer loss. If we do not, we get stuck, and our pain goes on and on ruling our lives. We become paralyzed, we cannot go on to new life, to the ability to love fully." "Yes but," said I, an expert in yes-butting, "we would be celebrating his life! The tree would be a reminder of his life, not a hanging on." A sigh from George. "Perhaps you could see it that way, but believe me, you must say a true `Goodbye'." I wasn't ready to abandon the pine tree. George saw it in my eyes, and went on, "You know, the wise Jews have a ritual around death. They `sit Shiva,' dressed in black, sometimes wailing, which is pretty weird to us who are not Jewish, but actually it is healthy. They

320

do official mourning for designated periods, in essence demanding of the bereaved that they buckle down and get through the process of grieving in a formal, recognized, and most importantly, supported way. We should be so wise." I sat dead still, contemplating the kind of comforting possibility of sitting Shiva. "You surely believe that Pete's soul will soar upwards when he leaves us, don't you?" "Of course," I replied, reaching for that comfort. "Well, think of him, rejoicing, celebrating, that he has been set free from cystic fibrosis, that he is in a new and wondrous reality. Think of how it will be for him if he looks down and sees his most beloved people surrendering to grief, trapped in it instead of rejoicing for him and sharing in his new freedom and joy."

A memory flashed into my mind. After my little son Jack died of cystic fibrosis, I wept every day for nearly a year. One day, he came back. I could neither hear nor see him, but his presence was powerful and real. He conveyed an exalted and exultant joy, indescribable and freeing. I shared his joy, as much as my small, earth-bound heart was able, and I realized it would be so with Pete. Peace filled the room, and a numinous sort of fog floated into our souls. George smiled, hugged me, and our deal was sealed.

Pete taught me how to play chess. The challenge and excitement of plotting moves gave my brain the sort of rush that good exercise gave the body and I loved it. Alas, Pete was better than I, and beat me consistently. "Mom, I get really bored, winning all the time. You are dumb as a post and no challenge at all, so let's quit."

I was hurt and I was not either dumb as a post. We began a game new to both of us, "Master Mind." I made a slick move and Pete said, "You dirty rat! You're going to pay for that dastardly deal!" He then made a move, an evil glint in his beady eye, and I said, "Oh no you don't, buster, you are a dead man on this one!" "Not yet I'm not!" he snarled, and I gulped, "I don't think that is what I meant to say." "Yeah, Mom, you are really short on tact," and I shot back, "Well, old Pete, at least you know where you got it." He wouldn't give quarter, and said, "And that's not the only bummer I inherited from you!" "Touché, and ouch! We had better shut up and play."

And so we would, there beside the St. Vrain River. The Sacred Rustling Cottonwoods, sun playing in fluttering leaves, sheltered us. The river sang its soft song, as it danced over its rocky bed. Loveliness drifted all around, embracing us, God communicating without language. I said, "I think in Heaven they don't use words, they just use music." "Yeah," Pete replied, then, after a long silence, "Once when I was doing an acid trip, I SAW music. That's how it probably is in Heaven." And so we sat there in the lovely springtime, munching Cheetos, sipping Coke, listening to, and feeling God.

Slowly, the time came when we could no longer take our little trips. Pete had to be helped to the bathroom, helped with everything. The anger that had made him so difficult, had alienated friends and wounded his family, evaporated. As he struggled toward death, there was no longer energy for anger as both energy and time became precious. The spirits that were whispering to him, consciously or subcon-

322

sciously, conveyed to him that every wisp of strength he had he must spend on forgiveness, acceptance and love.

The family who could, came from far and near to be with Pete before he left us. Friends were not much in evidence, possibly unwilling to face "the skull that haunts mankind," death. Pete was bothered not at all, and said, "Dying isn't that big a deal." Family, and a few true friends, gave all the support possible. Katrina Mora, Doreen's beautiful daughter, came often to sit with Pete. She is a friend forever.

Our dear friend, Ann Brown, who had taught Pete through St. John's grammar school, said, "You and Pete need to cry together." It just would not happen for either of us. Perhaps we felt if we started, we wouldn't be able to stop, and we would drown in our tears. So we stayed on the beach in an illusion of escape from crashing waves of grief.

One evening Pete said, "Mom, we need to talk." We sat on his bed. We put our arms around each other, but no words would come, and we were silent, on the edge of some psychic cliff. If we spoke, would we crash in to the sea below? A train went by in the distance; its horn eerily announcing to the night that it was on its way. I said, "Listen, Pete—that sound, speeding through the night, going SOMEWHERE." As the whistle died away in the distance, Pete said, "That's how it is. A journey into the night. I have to make it alone." Alone, alone, alone. " I am not afraid. I am going to make my Great Leap soon." He lay down then, asked for his favorite music, softly. He asked me to rub his head, his neck, and his arms. He drifted off to sleep, and I dropped to the mattress on the floor beside his bed, too drained to think or to feel.

Day was just breaking when I awoke. Pete had left! Morning sun was shining in, shining benevolence on his still-warm body. His face glowed with peace. A wild and wonderful sense of him filled the room. He was flying around the ceiling, celebrating his escape from 24 years of illness and pain! How could we not celebrate with him?

The Funeral

So many of our friends, and almost all the Echeverrias, were Catholic; and as such, we were pretty well stuck with a funeral Mass, despite Pete's orders not to stoop to that, but we did manage a compromise. Peter and Leonard Urban were two priests who had been more or less banished to tiny Mead, Colorado, because, like us, they were heretics. They lived with two nuns who wore Levis along with the rest of us, and they preached merrily about freedom and the lushness of life, to be lived fully, as a gift from God. Our kind of people, of course. They were eager to plan a heretical celebration of Pete's Great Leap.

Pete had asked that we hold his wake in our back yard with its expansive green lawn, beautiful big trees, the little orchard of fruit trees and the grove of 17 aspens he had planted. A magical place, it would be perfect. We set up long tables and lots of chairs. People began to arrive, loading the groaning boards with delectable goodies. They filled ice tubs with the beer, wine, whiskey and champagne that Pete had said we had better have plenty of, and we certainly did.

About the time the priests arrived to start their version of a funeral Mass, the sky grew dark. Thunder and lightning began rumbling and flashing, and it started to sprinkle. Joseph was sitting next to me in the front row and I heard him growl, "Pete, cut that out!" The rain stopped during the Mass created to celebrate Transition, rather than mourn death, and the sun broke through the magnificent thunderheads. Pete put on a sunset that shouted GLORY!

Love swirled warmly all around us. We could sense the love of Those Above; including Pete, and our angels. As the Mass was completed, someone shouted, "LOOK! It's Pete!" and we turned to see a brilliant rainbow arching over our yard, its two ends on the walls. There was no doubt that it was Pete's spirit announcing, "Hale, Farewell, and Alleluia!" Gasps and whispers sped through the gathering, "It's Pete!" "It's Pete!" So we drank to him, we drank to him, with all our hearts, as his poem had instructed.

A band, friends of the kids, played, and the dancing, whooping and hollering commenced. The darndest people danced with each other—nuns from St. John's kicking up their heels, old people boogying away, little kids bounding about like fawns, all of us swept up in Pete's joy, and in the holiness of our heresy. The food was wonderful, and the champagne, beer and drinks were plentiful and the party was famous for years as gloriously uninhibited. Pete would have it no other way.

Often during the events our family had, the police turned up just to check on us. This time they waved a greeting and drove on. Maybe they hoped that with one less of us things would calm down. How wrong they were. That's another story.

Pete's ashes were delivered in a box that I have still. The blanket he was taken away in was returned, and I embroidered his name on it, so we would remember always. I put the box in my carry-on bag and flew to Phoenix, Pete under the seat in front of me.

Mike Coffinger, the Wickenburg undertaker, had gone to school and camped in Havasupai Canyon with my brothers and me. As an old friend, he bent rules and allowed us the burial Pete had requested, except that Pete was ash instead of an un-embalmed corpse. At dawn our immediate family, Andy Pilkington, Granny, John and Dana Burden, got in the back of Uncle Pete's ancient, blue, Chevy pickup—it seemed the only adequate vehicle available, and somehow it was perfect—and Uncle Pete drove us to the cemetery. Mike had dug a hole next to little Jack's grave.

We made a nest of flowers in the bottom, poured Pete's ashes in, covered them with more flowers, and then took turns shoveling dirt in on top. A just-past full moon was setting in the West, as the sun announced a new day, a New Time, coming up over the mountains East of Wickenburg. Doves sang their love songs, quail darted about, calling to each other, and five deer appeared, wandering across the cemetery edge, quite close to us. Someone said, "Let's sing something," and we stumbled through "Morning Has Broken," gave that up, joined hands for the Lord's Prayer, and said our last good-byes. I could hardly leave, but we couldn't just stay there. We hopped in Uncle Pete's truck and left.

The day flew by with most of us playing water polo in Uncle

Pete's pool. He made us Johnny Cakes, good comfort food, except he forgot the salt and he didn't have any butter, jam or syrup. Someone dashed to Safeway for survival rations.

That night we had a party for the many friends and a thundering herd of Echeverrias who were not at our small, dawn ceremony. The Echeverrias came bearing delectable Basque desserts, steaks were grilled, food was served, and, again, there was more than enough alcohol flowing. A merry enough time was had, there on Apache Flats, the last of the family's Remuda Ranch land.

People seemed to find it difficult to talk to me, which was a relief. What I really wanted was to watch the stars come out, glittering as they do in Arizona's desert sky. I wanted to see the just-past full moon, rising up over the ridge to the East, shining benevolent gold down on us, and to smell the greasewood, see the mesquite trees making leaf patterns of black lace against the moon-lit sky, and to feel the good dust beneath my feet. That's where Pete was, where God was, where peace and joy were.

Paul brought me an envelope early the next morning, before we all flew back to Colorado. He said, "Pete gave me this right before he died, and told me to give it to you as soon as he was gone. I read it, and thought it would be better if I waited until after the funeral was over. Forgive me, old Pete, you wild man," he added, looking skyward. I opened it and read it, my heart in my throat, my head spinning. Had Paul given it to me as Pete instructed, I might have thrown sanity to the winds, looked both ways, broken the law and followed his wishes.

It contained detailed instructions for how he REALLY wanted his funeral. We were to forget our "stupid" caution, and take him to McCarty Canyon Ranch, immediately, just as he was when he died. A funeral pyre of good Wyoming wood was to be piled up in the pasture near the ranch house. Like a Viking warrior, he was to be draped in white robes, raised up and placed on top, and then each of us was to light a torch, and set it all ablaze. We were to dance around it, in a circle, like Druids, cheering and chanting until he was turned to ash. What a glorious idea, and only Pete, the Rocket Man, Shot From Earth To The Moon, could have come up with it.

That night I held the letter to my heart, and in the silence and the dark, I looked up at Pete's moon and asked, "What next?"

To be notified when the conclusion of Sophie's three-part

memoir is released, or to order Part I,

When in Doubt Step on the Gas,

please email sophnano@gmail.com.

When in Doubt and *Look Both Ways Before Breaking*

the Law may also be ordered directly from

amazon.com.

10346372R00210

Made in the USA
Charleston, SC
27 November 2011